TEN-MINUTE PLAYS
— THE —
COMEDY
COLLECTION

ANDREW BISS

ENTR'ACTE
EDITIONS

2017

Original cover image © Rolffimages
Cover design by Ernest Waggenheim

First Edition

ISBN: 1978322283
ISBN-13: 978-1978322288

"Of course I talk to myself. I like a good speaker and I appreciate an intelligent audience."

— Dorothy Parker

TABLE OF CONTENTS

INTRODUCTION

The rise in popularity of the ten-minute play over the past twenty or so years is truly remarkable. Once viewed as a little-regarded subgenre of its older brother (or sister) the one-act play, it has since become ubiquitous across the theatrical landscape. The one-act play festival – once so dominant in theatre communities throughout the country – has since been dethroned by its upstart sibling – and for good reason.

It's not difficult to understand the appeal of the ten-minute play for audiences. Watching a program of perhaps three or four one-act plays, each with a running time of between thirty to forty-five minutes, is perfectly fine as long as you're enjoying the works being presented. But if you're sitting through one that's rather dull or boring – or just flat-out bad – that forty-five minutes is going to feel like an eternity. In a program of ten-minute plays, however, the odd dud will fly by in no time, with the prospect of an undiscovered gem just around the corner.

They're also good for theatres and actors, offering a wide selection of programming options and a far greater number of roles available to the local acting community.

But of course, a ten-minute play isn't an actual *play* unless it adheres to certain criteria, namely having a beginning, middle and end, a narrative arc that connects those points, a strong sense of conflict, and well-defined characters – without them it's simply a sketch. Needless to say, fitting all of that into a time frame of around 600 seconds is no mean feat, which is why the prestige of the well-written ten-minute play has grown along with its prevalence.

The plays in this particular collection are all comedies...a fact you'll have undoubtedly deduced from its less-than-cryptic title. But that is not to say that they're all similar in style. Some have their roots in realism, while others willfully and wantonly upend theatrical customs and conventions. Some are playful and lighthearted, while others hew closer to the realm of dark comedy. But whatever their milieu, they all share one common goal: to entertain and amuse.

The vast majority of these plays have enjoyed multiple productions around the country – and indeed the world in some cases – garnering critical plaudits and awards along the way. Now, with this publication, they'll have the opportunity to find new friends and enthusiasts...and it's sincerely hoped that you'll become one of them.

The Craft

THE CRAFT

1M/1F

It's Act 2, Scene 3 in another night's performance of a less-than-riveting romantic drama. As the two young leads navigate their turgid love scene, employing all their dramatic skills in an attempt to breathe life into their two-dimensional characters, another, far more gripping story is unfolding just beneath the surface. Despite a mutual loathing of each other, a devotion to the craft ensures that the show will go on; but the inner dialogues that play out inside each of them reveal a far different narrative than the one being played out on the stage.

The Craft premiered at the Off Cut festival at Riverside Studios, London, in 2011, produced by In Company Theatre.

CHARACTERS

ACTOR 1: A cocky, bravura exterior masks the frustrated, insecure actor within. Male. 20s/30s.

ACTOR 2: Centered, professional, committed to her work, with an aversion to suffering fools. Female. 20s/30s.

SETTING & TIME

SETTING: A stage.

TIME: The present.

Playwright's note: This play contains very little *actual* stage direction, as almost all of it is revealed by the actors themselves through their spoken inner dialogues. It should also be noted that since the dialogue in this play consists entirely of the actors' inner dialogues, neither of them at any time is actually hearing what the other is saying. Furthermore, both actors should – as far as possible – attempt to match their expressions and body language to what is being experienced by the characters in the play-within-the-play, rather than reflecting the emotions of the actors' inner dialogues.

At rise: There is a small table placed downstage center, with a chair to the right of it, and a small bench seat to the left. ACTOR 1 enters.

ACTOR 1: Act Two, Scene Three. I enter from stage right...nervous but in character, cross to the chair placed downstage center, next to the small table, and sit. I look up, seemingly forlorn, and begin my brief soliloquy that speaks of the turmoil and heartache inside of me that was all-too-obviously telegraphed in the previous scene. (*Beat*) I direct it to the fourth wall, as if speaking to anyone and no one, *and yet...*some woman in the third or fourth row is wearing a blouse of a color so loud and garish that I find my peripheral vision is being constantly distracted by it, thus diminishing the gravitas of what I'm attempting to impart to the audience at large. God I hate her – she's really screwing this up for me. (*Beat*) I ignore her as best I can and concentrate on the words. Okay, I'm done. God, I hate her – she really threw me off. (*Beat*) I think my expression at the end really got them, though...despite the distraction of Coco the Clown in row C or D or wherever the hell she is. (*Beat*) All right then, darling, let's be having you...make your entrance please...*now.* (*Beat*) Christ, where is she? Come on, come on! (*Beat*) All right, don't panic. Try to look deep in thought, as if there's a very important inner dialogue raging inside of you – then maybe the audience will think it's all deliberate. (*Beat*) God, I could strangle her right now! *Where the hell is she?*

(*ACTOR 2 enters from stage left.*)

ACTOR 2: I enter hurriedly from stage left.

ACTOR 1: *At last!*

ACTOR 2: I run across the stage, desperately seeking the whereabouts of my one true love...even though I can see him sitting right there and would have to be half blind not to have spotted him immediately...*but*...this is theatre, so on I search, hoping, hoping, until...oh yes, there he is...my heart's desire...in the form of one of the most obnoxious and egotistical jerks I've ever had the misfortune of working with. I smile sweetly.

ACTOR 1: I suddenly become aware of her presence...and of the very dark circles under her eyes, which no amount of make-up was able to disguise, apparently. Out on the town with the director again last night, I'm assuming. My, what a far cry from the delicate little flower she's attempting to fob off on the audience right now. Drunken old slattern. I turn away, hurt.

ACTOR 2: I drop to my knees and beseech him. If he only knew why I had to rebuff him in the library in the previous scene. If he only knew of the deep dark secret I've been forced to keep hidden from him. If he only...if he only...if he'd only look me in the eye for just a second! I mean, come on, we're supposed to be doing this thing together. It's called acting. It's reacting as well as speaking, you know? I need something to work with here. Hello? Hello?

ACTOR 1: I wonder if there's any agents in the audience tonight. I invited six but none of them responded. Wait a second...that guy back there with the glasses looks like he might be. (*Beat*) On second thoughts, no...too hip. Useless bastards. I expect they were all "too busy." Yeah, too busy propping up some bar, getting wasted after a hard day's skimming cash off the backs of their clients' hard work. Parasites. They should be sat out there doing their job...scouting for talent...witnessing art. (*Beat*) Oh, look out – her big speech is about to end. And not before time. She milks that thing like a Jersey cow. (*Beat*) I look up at her with a mixture of pity and confusion, and demand that she tells me her deep dark secret so that I can feign shock and surprise for yet another evening.

ACTOR 2: Oh look, it does have eyes after all. Good evening and thank you for joining me. It's so nice to have company. So...you want to know my terrible secret, do you? All right, I'll tell you. It's an almost uncontrollable desire to see you stripped naked and strung up by your balls from the light rigging, with a large prop of my choosing rammed up that vain, self-important and utterly talentless asshole of yours. But...since that's unlikely to transpire and not actually in the text, I suppose I'd better stick with the scripted version. (*Beat*) She covers her face with her hands, dreading his reaction to what she is about to disclose.

ACTOR 1: Yes, cover it up, dear – it's hard staring into those dark, puffy eyes for too long. I feel like I'm sharing a scene with a panda bear. (*Beat*) And if there *are* any agents out there tonight, I hope they're taking note, because *this* is acting. Not only am I having to navigate this scene alone with Ling-Ling here, but I mean, really – she had an abortion two years ago after a brief romp in the rhododendrons with the former gardener? I mean, who writes this crap? I'm supposed to be shocked and appalled by this revelation? It's hardly the stuff of Grand Guignol. Now, if she'd been raped by her father and given birth to a hideously deformed, inbred monstrosity that she kept chained to a post behind the summerhouse, *then…then* we'd have a revelation…*then* we'd have something to work with. But no, it's just your average, plain vanilla abortion saga, in response to which – and to great effect, using every skill at my disposal – I fix her with a steely gaze that betrays neither outrage nor compassion.

ACTOR 2: I pause briefly, looking into his eyes to see if my words have been met with pity or loathing. (*Beat*) As it turns out, it's neither. It's that same vacant, idiotic expression he wears every time the director gives him a note – he tries to pretend he's understood, but in truth just looks lobotomized. And his parents, with the benefit of hindsight, would probably agree with me now that that might have been the best option. (*Beat*) I express lots of guilt, etcetera, and explain how my father forced me into it.

ACTOR 1: An abortion? I'll tell you what an abortion is – this script. Hard to believe it got a first production, let alone a revival. I should be doing Mamet or Pinter or Shepard, not this potboiling drivel.

(*Pause.*)

ACTOR 2: Oh Christ, he's forgotten his lines – and *always* at the same spot.

ACTOR 1: If I had an agent I wouldn't have to do crap like

this. I'd get the roles I deserve…meaty ones…in juicy scripts…not this crap.

ACTOR 2: He has – he's forgotten his lines again!

ACTOR 1: God, I hate agents.

ACTOR 2: God, you *idiot!*

ACTOR 1: Useless bastards.

ACTOR 2: Think, you *idiot*, think!

ACTOR 1: Wait a second – where are we? Oh shit, it's my line!

ACTOR 2: *Think!*

ACTOR 1: Um…um, um, um, um…oh yeah – the very sudden, very clunky, not to mention plot-convenient change of heart, where I quickly forgive all and reaffirm my undying love. Urgh!

ACTOR 2: *At last!* I could slap you sometimes, I *really* could.

ACTOR 1: As if anyone could ever love that…apart from another panda, I suppose.

ACTOR 2: Amateur!

ACTOR 1: Oh, and the director, of course…after he's had a few.

ACTOR 2: Tears of joy fill my eyes, as I cross stage left to the window and look out, as if to symbolize the new life and new beginning that now lay ahead. Hackneyed and cheesy, yes, but that's what's in the script, so that's what I must do.

ACTOR 1: I cross to her and grab her by the throat. (*Beat*) Heh, heh, heh – just kidding. I tap her gently on the shoulder.

ACTOR 2: I turn around, my heart overflowing, to face my dear true love. My dear, true, lobotomized-looking love.

ACTOR 1: I get down on one knee, and from my pocket I produce a small box.

ACTOR 2: My eyes light up. Could it be…could it truly be…

ACTOR 1: Empty?

ACTOR 2: Oh shit!

ACTOR 1: Oh no!

ACTOR 2: You complete moron!

ACTOR 1: I swear it was there earlier. I swear it was. I checked…I think.

ACTOR 2: All right, don't panic, you idiot, just mime it.

ACTOR 1: Maybe it fell out. Maybe it's in my pocket. Perhaps I should check. No, I can't – the audience would know for sure then – it'd be obvious.

10

ACTOR 2: Just *mime* it.

ACTOR 1: What am I gonna put on her finger?

ACTOR 2: *Mime it!*

ACTOR 1: I'll just mime it.

ACTOR 2: He slips the engagement ring onto her finger, which she then lovingly admires – whilst deftly using her other hand to block its view from the audience – and proceeds to tell him how her heart is full of…well, actually, a death wish at this point.

ACTOR 1: That was quick thinking. The audience didn't suspect a thing. See, I don't panic in a crisis. That's the mark of a professional. You're learning from the best here, Ling-Ling.

ACTOR 2: Which now brings us to the sadly inevitable – the moment in the play that tortures my mind and churns my stomach eight times a week…the kiss. She turns her head to one side, coquettishly.

ACTOR 1: All right, Olivier, eat your heart out. I hope you're watching, wherever you are, because this, my friend, is the highest mountain an actor has ever had to climb. This is what separates the men from the boys, the hams from the Hamlets, for this is the moment where – after summoning every last ounce of strength and courage – I am called upon to…lock lips with bamboo breath.

ACTOR 2: Make it convincing, but make it *quick*.

ACTOR 1: I am fearless. I am an actor. I can do anything. Even this. He grabs the furry beast by its shoulders, making his intentions unmistakable.

ACTOR 2: She appears coy and vulnerable, her lower lip quivering slightly in anticipation of what she knows is to come. Her stomach, on the other hand, is gripped by nausea and revulsion...her head by a duty to the craft.

ACTOR 1: All right, Ling-Ling, here I come. And there'd better not be any director residue left on those lips – from his mouth or otherwise.

ACTOR 2: Bracing herself, she doggedly repeats her mantra: It's Jude Law, it's Jude Law, it's Jude law, it's Jude–

(They kiss for several moments, before ACTOR 1 releases ACTOR 2 from his embrace.)

ACTOR 2: ...Law.

ACTOR 1: Done! He emerges unscathed, and yet another night's meager wages are earned in full. They should give medals to some actors, not awards. (*Beat*) He stands before her with a look of pride...as well he should after that feat.

ACTOR 2: She strokes his cheek affectionately...while resisting the overwhelming urge to wipe her mouth with the back of her hand, and imagining the poor creatures that have had to endure that revolting experience in real life...assuming there's actually been any.

ACTOR 1: He takes her hand and leads her stage right to the bench seat.

ACTOR 2: Why is he going so damned fast? The director's told him about this *so* many times! I'll trip and break my neck one of these days.

ACTOR 1: He gestures for her to sit.

ACTOR 2: She sits.

ACTOR 1: He sits and places his arm around her...and proceeds with the cloying speech about his plans for their future together, and how happy they'll be, and of the children she'll bear him...literally, in this case – half-man, half-bear.

ACTOR 2: She leans her head tenderly against his shoulder...and contemplates the true meaning of paying ones dues, knowing that one day...one day, when she's a sought after actress of fame and repute, all of this – every last unctuous, frustrating, degrading moment she's ever had to endure – will all have been worth it.

ACTOR 1: He holds her close to him...and waits impatiently for the lights to come down. (*Beat*) Wait a second...did I turn my lights off when I pulled in here tonight? Oh no...I don't think I did. Oh shit...*shit!* Hurry the hell up with those damn lights, will you? I've gotta get out of here *now!* Come on, come on!

ACTOR 2: Thank God he gets murdered by my father in the next scene. She smiles contentedly...as the lights fade down...to black.

END OF PLAY

Kitchen Sink Drama

KITCHEN SINK DRAMA

2F

Elaine's husband has made a lurid confession that's thrown her neat and tidy, albeit dreary existence into complete turmoil. Seeking solace and guidance, she decides to share her shocking discovery with her estranged, capricious sister, Joy. What the unsuspecting Joy doesn't realise, however, is that she's about to make a shocking discovery of her own.

Kitchen Sink Drama premiered at Manhattan Theatre Source, New York, in 2009, produced by Mind The Gap Theatre.

CHARACTERS

ELAINE: World-weary with an acerbic edge that belies a timid core. Rather homespun in appearance but not unattractive. 20s/40s.

JOY: Elaine's sister. A self-possessed, independent thinker. Very attractive, stylish and brutally forthright. 20s/40s.

SETTING & TIME

SETTING: The kitchen of Elaine's home, lodged somewhere in the Home Counties of England.

TIME: The present.

At rise: ELAINE *is sitting in a chair at the kitchen table, book in hand, snacking from a bowl of something on the table. Momentarily the sound of a doorbell is heard.* ELAINE, *in a state of agitation, rushes to answer the door.*

ELAINE: *(Off)* Oh, Joy! Thank God! I've been waiting an eternity. I was starting to think you'd gone all peculiar on me, too. It's been an eon at least since I called.

(JOY enters, speaking in rapid-fire sentences, followed by ELAINE.)

JOY: Darling, my apologies, you must forgive me, but it's Wednesday, as you know – the day I have to take Stephen's brats to the park – hideous, I know, but what can you do? And so there I am, sitting on this hideously uncomfortable wooden bench that's covered in lichen and bird shit, being subjected to the most appalling high-pitched squeals and laughter emanating from those pre-pubescent monsters from Stephen's squalid little pre-me marriage, wondering what the hell I'd done to deserve it all, when I attempt – in desperation – to make contact with the outside world and check my messages, and wouldn't you know it…the damned phone's out of juice. So, then I have to drag these two creatures, kicking and screaming needless to say, to the nearest wine bar where I can plug in and recharge – me and the bloody phone – them crying and sobbing the whole three hours, of course – even though I'd bought them more magazines and fizzy drinks than you could possibly imagine – until I finally get a signal, got your hideous message, unloaded the brats back onto Stephen and charged over here as if my life depended on it. So how are you, darling? Well, obviously you're feeling completely hideous – but, I mean, other than that? Is everything all right?

ELAINE: Yes, everything's fine, really...other than that.

JOY: Well, that's a relief at least. Thank God for small mercies, I say. *(Beat)* So...what's the problem?

ELAINE: It's Graham.

JOY: Oh God, not again. What is it now? Don't tell me...you found another brown stain in his underwear.

ELAINE: No, Joy, it's...it's far more disturbing, I'm afraid.

JOY: Then what color is it?

ELAINE: It isn't a color. It has nothing to do with his underwear. Well...not really...I mean, it might do...in some ways...but not really...as far as I can tell.

JOY: Darling, I do apologize, but I've had a very long and very arduous day, so I'm afraid you're going to have to be substantially more specific if this conversation is to hold my attention. Now, does Graham's underwear factor in to your predicament or doesn't it?

(Beat.)

ELAINE: No.

JOY: Good, now that's clear, at least. So what does?

(Beat.)

ELAINE: His…his lover.

JOY: Oh, God – I knew it!

ELAINE: How did you know?

JOY: I don't know…just one of those things one says, I suppose. *(Beat)* Are you positive?

ELAINE: Yes, he's told me everything.

JOY: That was very forthright of him. Quite out of character, if you'll forgive my saying so, but there it is.

ELAINE: No, no, completely. Under duress, of course.

JOY: Of course. And what's her name?

ELAINE: It's not a "her".

JOY: What do you mean, "It's not a her"?

ELAINE: I mean, it's a "him".

JOY: Well, of course it's a "him". If it's not a "her" then there's not much else it could be, is there?

ELAINE: Then why ask?

JOY: I don't know – just one of those things one says, I suppose.

ELAINE: And?

JOY: And what?

ELAINE: Aren't you appalled?

JOY: No.

ELAINE: Why ever not?

JOY: Should I be?

ELAINE: He's having an affair.

JOY: With a man.

ELAINE: Precisely.

JOY: Precisely.

ELAINE: Joy, I'm your sister – I'm reaching out to you – at least try to grab my bloody hand!

JOY: But I am, darling. You just told me he's having an affair with a man.

ELAINE: Exactly.

JOY: So, why worry?

ELAINE: Why worry!

JOY: Yes. In fact, you should be pleased.

ELAINE: Pleased!

JOY: Yes – that it's a man.

> *(Beat.)*

ELAINE: *(Bemused)* I'm...I'm sorry, I don't follow.

JOY: Well, darling, if he's having an affair with another man then there's really nothing to worry about, is there? I mean, I'm assuming, of course, the marriage is sexless?

ELAINE: *(Defensively)* No more than the norm.

JOY: Well, there you are.

ELAINE: Where?

JOY: Where you should be.

ELAINE: I still don't understand.

JOY: Look, darling, he's only human, after all – hard to imagine sometimes, but there you are. And more to the point, he has needs along with the rest of us – though frankly, that's even harder to imagine.

ELAINE: Joy, how can you be so blasé about it? This is my life…in crisis!

JOY: Oh, for God's sake stop going on like some button-downed hausfrau. Just stop for a second, take a deep breath, and have a good hard look at yourself: You're of a certain age; you and Graham have been married for…God knows how long…

ELAINE: Seemingly forever.

JOY: Seemingly forever; you no longer find each other sexually appealing – and on the odd occasion you feel obliged to do so, it's more than likely forced and horrid; there's doubtless very little left in that burnt out ember of love that, with great force of mind, I can only vaguely imagine you once shared, and what little conversation you continue to exchange is almost certainly argumentative and combative, or else so dull and predictable that both of you have trouble summoning the energy to respond, since you both already assume to know what the other's going to say before the sentence has hardly begun. Am I right?

(Beat.)

ELAINE: What if you were?

JOY: So, what do you expect? These things are going to happen.

ELAINE: Well, perhaps they are, but…but I still don't understand how you can be so matter-of-fact about Graham being with another man.

JOY: Darling, he's just scratching an itch. You know men and sex; it's like going to the lavatory – they'll do it just about anywhere when the urge is strong enough.

ELAINE: *(Unconvinced)* I suppose so.

JOY: Of course so. Look at the prison system, for God's sake – it's a virtual World's Fair of heterosexual buggery.

ELAINE: Even so…it's still not right…it's still cheating.

JOY: Oh, for Christ's sake, listen to you – prattling on like some horn-rimmed hangover from the 1950's. It's a part of life, for heaven's sake – haven't you figured that out yet? I mean, how old are you? *(Beat)* Anyway, it doesn't count with another man – it's just sex. If he were banging some opportunistic little sex kitten I'd see more cause for concern. I mean, let's face it, you're losing what few looks you once had – I hate to say it, darling, but there it is – your personality's a non-starter, and you've absolutely no trade skills. Your entire future would hinge upon some greasy little solicitor. But, luckily for you, Graham isn't banging some little kitten, he's merely…exercising his options.

ELAINE: I don't care what you say, it's still not right. And besides, why should he be the one to have all the excitement? It's me whose life is in a rut. I'm the one stuck in this miserable bloody house all day, summoning ways to fill this void that I laughingly call "my life". I'm the one starving for a little diversion, for God's sake.

JOY: So, what exactly is it that bothers you– the gender preference or the humping in general?

ELAINE: Both. *(Pause)* The humping.

JOY: *(Impatiently)* Then you've only yourself to blame.

ELAINE: What a ridiculous, and, may I say, very hurtful thing to say.

JOY: Elaine, life does not come to you – you must go to it. If you want more excitement in your life, then I'm afraid you're going to have to make a little bit more of an effort – unless, of course, you're content to mope around here like some Chekhovian drudge for the rest of your life.

ELAINE: What are you suggesting?

JOY: Nothing. I'm merely pointing out that Graham – in all his Grahamness – has somehow managed to inject a little colour into his drab life whilst still maintaining the status quo. If you lack the initiative to do the same then that's your business, but for Christ's sake stop pointing your finger at other people like some miserable martyred blob of inertia.

ELAINE: You're saying I should cheat on him?

JOY: I refer back to my last statement.

ELAINE: So, you are?

JOY: *(Her patience nearing an end)* Oh, for God's sake, Elaine –

"cheat"? What the hell does that mean? What sort of Sesame Street mentality do you live by? It's just a word. A word that describes not living by the rules, and if you choose to live the rest of your life living by the rules, then...then, best of luck, darling.

ELAINE: *(Stridently)* I have always tried to live my life in a—

JOY: You live your life in an emotionless, sexless marriage. You don't have a loving relationship, you have a husband and a house – both of which are semi-detached – and if you're so hamstrung by your own misguided Girl Scout morality that you can't see the wood for the trees, then...then stop leaving hysterical messages on my cell phone.

ELAINE: *(Reprovingly)* I wonder what Stephen would say if he could hear you now.

JOY: Probably exactly what I'm saying.

ELAINE: I doubt that very much.

JOY: Do you? Well, in that case, why don't you ask one of his tarts...or better yet, ask one of mine.

ELAINE: You mean, you...both of you...

JOY: Get it? Yes. We don't involve each other in it. To all intents and purposes we live a perfectly normal married life. But we've both found ways to...fill in the blanks without spoiling the puzzle.

ELAINE: Exactly – you cheat at the puzzle.

JOY: We both take a peek in the dictionary once in a while, when the other's not looking. It's not cheating, it's...keeping the game in play. Look, it's not that complicated. In fact, it's not complicated at all. I can't imagine living my life without Stephen in it, nor he me, presumably. We wish to remain together. Therefore, we acknowledge and accept those occasional liberties that will enable us to continue doing so. Make sense?

ELAINE: But you...you seemed so content, you and Stephen?

JOY: We are, that's just it!

ELAINE: But, doesn't he...

JOY: No.

ELAINE: Aren't you...

JOY: No.

ELAINE: But he has to...

JOY: No, he doesn't – and neither do I.

> *(Beat.)*

ELAINE: But it can't be as easy as all that. Life's not that simple.

JOY: Life is very simple, darling: you live, you breathe, you die – that's it. Whatever you choose to do with the rest of it is entirely up to you. It's only as complicated as you want to make it.

(Pause.)

ELAINE: I suppose…I suppose you could have a point.

JOY: Could? Of course I do. Just because Stephen doesn't like sushi doesn't mean I can't drop into Mr. Takimoto's and nibble on his uni once in a while, does it?

ELAINE: Well…yes, but–

JOY: Anyway, Graham's opened the door; the rest is up to you. Only, if you choose to do nothing, for God's sake stop moaning on at me about it – I've enough on my plate.

(Pause.)

ELAINE: I'm not sure what I shall do. I need time to think…I think. But I will admit that you've forced me to look at things from a…a different perspective…one I hadn't considered. And I am grateful for it, Joy – really I am. And I know you think that I dislike you underneath, because you were always the pretty one and I was always second best, but I don't…I don't, Joy. I've never begrudged you that. Even though you were cruel sometimes. And your opinions really do mean a lot to me…and I promise I shall give them very serious consideration.

JOY: Haven't a clue what you're talking about, but as far as the last part's concerned – good.

ELAINE: And, God forbid, if Graham should ever have a similar dream, then I...well, I shall... take decisive measures.

(Beat.)

JOY: What?

ELAINE: I said, I shall take decisive measures.

JOY: Did you say, "dream"?

ELAINE: Yes.

JOY: What dream?

ELAINE: Graham's dream – about having sex with another man.

JOY: *(Incredulous)* It was a dream?

ELAINE: Yes. *(Beat)* Did I not mention that?

JOY: *(Furious)* No! No, you damn well didn't!

ELAINE: Oh...well, it was.

JOY: For Christ's sake! You mean I scrambled over here like a bat out of hell, after a day of sheer bloody torture, thinking you were on the edge of an abyss, all because of some stupid bloody dream?

ELAINE: I'm sorry, I…I found it very disturbing.

JOY: You're the one that's disturbed, if you ask me! For God's sake, the man has a subconscious fantasy about sex with another man and you start flailing around like some demented octopus! Christ, I hate you sometimes, I really do!

ELAINE: Joy, he performed acts upon him…he told me.

JOY: So-bloody-what?

ELAINE: He allowed this young man to…to enter him!

JOY: It was a dream!

ELAINE: He enjoyed it!

JOY: *(Standing)* All right, that's it – I've had enough. I'm sorry, Elaine, but Stephen's brats and middle-class hysteria all in one day, it's…it's just too much. I'm leaving.

(JOY crosses to the door L.)

ELAINE: *(Beseechingly)* Oh, Joy! Joy!

JOY: *(Turning in the doorway)* No, Elaine. No! I have just imparted very personal details and aspects regarding my private life to you because, as your sister, I felt a duty and an obligation to do so, since you'd led me to believe that you were in a strange place and needed guidance. As it turns out, you're insane and I'm a fool, so let's just cut our losses. Good afternoon.

(*JOY exits. ELAINE hurries to the doorway and calls after her.*)

ELAINE: But Joy, I haven't told you the worst part – he made Graham pregnant!

JOY: (*Off*) Lunatic!

(*The front door is heard slamming. ELAINE turns back to the room with a look of wide-eyed apprehension.*)

ELAINE: With triplets!

(*The lights fade to BLACK.*)

END OF PLAY

The Skewed Picture

THE SKEWED PICTURE

1M/1F

Bob and Betty have settled in for a quiet night at home. That is, until Bob makes a startling discovery that has the potential to reshape their entire existence…or at least their living room. The realization that a parallel universe could be staring them in the face forces them to question just who exactly these people might be, and more importantly, why they're there?

The Skewed Picture premiered at The Vortex Theatre's Don't Blink! International Play Festival, in Albuquerque, New Mexico, in 2011.

CHARACTERS

BETTY: An avid cruciverbalist. 20s/60s.

BOB: An avid reader. 20s/60s.

SETTING & TIME

SETTING: A living room.

TIME: The present.

At rise: BETTY *and* BOB *are discovered sitting on a sofa, downstage C.* BETTY *is studiously working on a crossword puzzle, while* BOB *is completely engrossed in a book that he's reading. After several moments,* BOB *suddenly and quite dramatically slams the book shut, causing* BETTY *to jump.*

BETTY: Oh!

BOB: That is absolutely, positively, undeniably the most astonishing thing that I have ever read in my entire life – ever!

BETTY: Yes, well…do you think you could do it a bit more quietly, please?

BOB: Astounding!

BETTY: (*Refocused back on her puzzle*) Mmm…

BOB: Earth shattering!

BETTY: That's nice.

BOB: It's almost…too much to get my head around.

BETTY: So's twenty-two across. (*Beat*) What's an eight-letter word for "memory meltdown"?

BOB: This changes everything, Betty. Everything we ever thought we knew and understood about our existence has just been turned on its head and tossed out the window – it's that big!

BETTY: It's frustrating is what it is. Fancy having your memory fail you on a clue called "memory meltdown."

BOB: But Betty…don't you want to know my discovery?

BETTY: Oh. Oh, yes of course. (*Putting down her puzzle*) What is it, then?

BOB: Betty…are you familiar with…a parallel universe?

BETTY: It's popped up from time to time, yes.

BOB: It has?

BETTY: Yes. Every now and then.

BOB: (*Cautiously scanning the room*) Where, exactly?

BETTY: In the crossword.

BOB: Oh. No, no, no. Betty, what I'm asking is, are you able to fully comprehend what the existence of a parallel universe would actually mean in the true metaphysical sense?

BETTY: Um…I can't honestly say yes to that…so no.

BOB: No…no, because it's almost unthinkable, isn't it?

BETTY: Yes, I suppose so.

BOB: The implications of it are mind-blowing…frightening, even.

BETTY: What is it, then?

BOB: What it is, Betty…is a separate, entirely self-contained universe that coexists on the same parallel as our very own. Coexists, Betty. Just think about that.

BETTY: Another universe…right here?

BOB: Yes.

BETTY: In our living room?

BOB: Quite possibly.

BETTY: It must be quite a small one, then. Where is it, do you think?

BOB: Aha! That's the mystery. That's what we don't know.

BETTY: So how do you know it's there?

BOB: Oh, it's there all right. There's been all manner of research and studies done on this. Countless studies. It's undeniable. Irrefutable.

BETTY: But how did it get there?

BOB: Well, I, uh…as I understand it, it was, um…the result of a, uh…a quantum event.

BETTY: Which is what?

BOB: That, I'm, um…not *entirely* sure of, but I do have it on good authority.

BETTY: Oh.

BOB: Remarkable, isn't it? When I sat down here on this couch with you not thirty minutes ago, I thought it was just the two of us settling down to exercise our grey matter for a while. Little did *I* know.

BETTY: I still don't know.

BOB: Betty, it's all changed, don't you see?

BETTY: What's changed?

BOB: *Everything.*

BETTY: (*Cautiously scanning the room*) It all looks the same to me.

BOB: Ah, yes, it may look the same to the naked eye, but that doesn't mean that it is the same.

BETTY: Doesn't it?

BOB: Not at all – because now we know, don't we?

BETTY: Um...yes.

BOB: Now we're aware of that parallel universe. Here we are, Betty...sitting here, coexisting with it. Isn't it incredible?

BETTY: Mmm.

BOB: I wonder where it is, exactly. (*Beat*) Perhaps it's right here... (*Gesturing towards the fourth wall*) Right in front of our very eyes.

BETTY: But that's our wall.

BOB: Yes, yes, it may look like our wall to you and me...

> (BOB *gets up from the sofa and places his hands flat against the fourth wall.*)

BOB: It may even feel like our wall...but perhaps it isn't our wall. Perhaps it's...a quantum event.

BETTY: Well, if it is a quantum event it's got our picture hanging on it.

BOB: Yes, and a little askew, if I'm not mistaken.

> (BOB *makes a small adjustment to the picture that hangs on the fourth wall.*)

BETTY: Are you sure about all this, Bob?

BOB: Never more certain.

BETTY: Because I just see a wall.

BOB: Yes, we both see a wall. It's what we're meant to see. But if in fact, as I'm becoming increasingly convinced, this is not really a wall at all but a quantum event, then what we see before us could actually function as some sort of inter-universe two-way mirror.

BETTY: Oh.

BOB: Just imagine...right now, right as we speak, there could be someone – hell, there could be a whole roomful of people – just sitting there, staring at us.

BETTY: Why would they want to do that?

BOB: I've no idea.

> (*BETTY gets up from the sofa and stands next to BOB, staring at the fourth wall.*)

BETTY: Perhaps they're lonely?

BOB: Oh, I don't think so. I expect they're just curious.

BETTY: About us?

BOB: Yes.

BETTY: I don't know why...I wouldn't be.

BOB: Perhaps in observing us – in studying us – they're

hoping to see something of themselves in us, and consequently find a sort of catharsis in our shared experience. I think they're hoping to learn things from us that they can take away and apply to their own lives in their own universe.

BETTY: I don't think they'll learn very much watching you read a book and me do the crossword.

BOB: Well, perhaps not at this precise juncture, but, um…well, at other times…when we're more animated and, um…well, busy being us.

BETTY: Just a minute! You don't suppose this two-way mirror thing extends all the way to our bedroom and bathroom, do you? I wouldn't want them looking at us when we're…you know…exposed.

BOB: Oh my goodness, no. I don't imagine for a second that a quantum event would ever be caught dabbling in smut.

BETTY: Thank heavens. Gave me a bit of a turn just thinking of it.

BOB: No, I'm sure it's all aboveboard and confined only to this room. If there is anyone out there looking at us, I'm sure they have absolutely no interest in probing our more sensitive areas.

(*Pause.*)

BETTY: I wonder if they're forced to do it.

BOB: To come and look at us?

BETTY: Yes.

BOB: Oh, I wouldn't think so. (*Beat*) One or two of them, perhaps.

BETTY: They could be. They could live in some sort of totalitarian state where they're forced into rooms and made to look at ordinary people going about their business, no matter how boring it gets. Perhaps it's a form of torture?

BOB: Oh dear me, Betty, you *are* putting a bleak spin on things, aren't you? (*Beat*) No, I prefer to think of it as something...cultural.

BETTY: Cultural? Us?

BOB: Well...not *us* necessarily – although I do believe my choice of reading material does denote the hallmarks of an enlightened mind – but in general, yes, I wouldn't be surprised if many of them are gazing at us in search of some form of...edification.

BETTY: That pops up now and then, too.

BOB: What does?

BETTY: Edification...in the crossword.

BOB: Ah.

BETTY: I always think it has something to do with eating, for some reason. (*Beat*) I wonder what they look like.

BOB: Just like us, I expect.

BETTY: What do you mean, like...clones?

BOB: No, no, just regular people...all types, all stripes.

BETTY: Mmm... (*Beat*) It's a bit eerie if you think about it, isn't it? I mean, even though it still looks like our wall, if I think about it long enough...well, I can almost feel them looking at me right now...feel their eyes all over me.

BOB: Steady on, Betty. No need for hysterics.

(*Pause.*)

BETTY: Here's a thought.

BOB: Hmm?

BETTY: Perhaps they're just looking to be entertained.

BOB: Oh, no! Oh my goodness me, no! No, no, no, no, no! This is...really, I'm...I am very disappointed in you, Betty...*very* disappointed.

BETTY: Well, they might.

BOB: How could you even contemplate such a thought? Here we are, knee-deep in quantum events and the warping

Excessive?No.

of space and time, and somehow you see fit to reduce everything down to the level of the boulevard. I find this *most* disturbing and *highly* inappropriate.

BETTY: It was just a thought.

BOB: They're probably all sophisticates and aesthetes with a hankering for the lofty. They wouldn't be looking for cheap entertainment or silly distractions. These poor people are probably *desperate* for some sort of meaningful cultural experience – I can almost feel it oozing from them. They're starved and they're looking to us for nourishment. And damn it, Betty, we're going to do everything within our power to make sure they get it.

BETTY: We are?

BOB: Yes, we are. We're going to give them all of the culture they'd ever dreamed of and more besides. We'll read the classics to them, every one of them; we'll recite poetry from Keats to Cummings; we'll play them Brahms and Beethoven; we'll reenact every play ever written in any language.

BETTY: Oh.

BOB: We'll sing operas to them; we'll show them our dance steps; we'll read them every thought of every philosopher that ever existed; we'll give them lectures in art history and seminars on mime. By God, Betty, by the time we're done with them, they'll be on their knees, *begging* for a way to thank us!

BETTY: Oh dear!

BOB: Right then, let's get to work. I say we start with some James Joyce. Now where did I put my copy of Finnegan's Wake?

BETTY: Um...

BOB: Did I leave it in the...no, no, not there. Perhaps I put it in the...no, I wouldn't have done that. Did I put it on top of the...but why on earth would I have put it there? Oh, this is all terribly frustrating! (*Beat*) Wait a second...I've just realized something.

BETTY: Oh?

BOB: Your crossword puzzle.

BETTY: Yes?

BOB: Twenty-two across...an eight-letter word for "memory meltdown."

BETTY: What?

BOB: Isn't it obvious?

BETTY: Is it?

BOB: Blackout!

BETTY: (*With great relief*) Blackout!

(BLACKOUT.)

END OF PLAY

A Flawed Character

A FLAWED CHARACTER

2 Any Age/Race/Gender Combination

The playwright creates the first character of his new play, but soon after the entire process grinds to a halt. As time marches on and the play continues to stagnate, the character's patience begins to wear thin. As frustration turns into animosity and antagonism, the playwright begins to realize that perhaps this is one relationship that was never meant to be. But what's a writer to do?

CHARACTERS

CHARACTER: A character in a play.

AUTHOR: Playwright of the aforementioned play.

SETTING & TIME

SETTING: A stage.

TIME: The present.

At rise: CHARACTER is discovered sitting at a table, head nestled in arms atop the table. On the other side of the table are a pen and a pad of paper. The chair opposite is empty. Presently, AUTHOR enters and sits down in the empty chair.

CHARACTER: *(Head raised from repose)* Well, well...the great author returns.

AUTHOR: So it would seem.

CHARACTER: I'd all but given up on you.

AUTHOR: I told you I'd be back as soon as I could.

CHARACTER: I thought you said you were going to the bathroom.

AUTHOR: I did.

CHARACTER: Oh. *(Beat)* Problems?

AUTHOR: I don't think that's any of your concern or a particularly appropriate question to ask. But since you have – no.

CHARACTER: I didn't mean intestinal ones; I was referring to the creative variety.

AUTHOR: Oh. (*Beat*) Well, the answer's still no. I simply became sidetracked by...by some other matters that...required my attention.

CHARACTER: I see. (*Beat*) Of course, in my day we called it procrastinating.

AUTHOR: What do you mean, "In my day"? You don't have a day. I just made you up. You're a character I created for my play, that's all.

CHARACTER: All right, all right, scratch that. Forget I said it.

AUTHOR: You *didn't* say it. Until I write it, you haven't said it.

CHARACTER: Oh, excuse me. I stand – sit – chastened and corrected.

AUTHOR: Good.

CHARACTER: After all, you're the one with the pen.

AUTHOR: Yes I am, and don't you forget it. (*Brandishing the pen*) This is mightier than the sword, remember?

CHARACTER: Yes, well, whilst I appreciate the metaphor, personally I know what I'd rather be holding if challenged to a duel.

AUTHOR: Well, since I have no intention of including any

duels, you don't have anything to worry about, do you?

CHARACTER: No, I suppose not. But if I were wielding a sword against some poor gimp holding a ballpoint pen, I don't think I'd have been particularly worried to begin with.

AUTHOR: Look, can we just forget about duels? There aren't going to be any. In fact, there'll be no violence of any kind in this work.

CHARACTER: No…nor much of anything, really.

AUTHOR: Excuse me?

CHARACTER: Well, what have you got so far?

AUTHOR: (*Hesitates*) You.

CHARACTER: Yes, of whom we know nothing.

AUTHOR: Not yet, because it's…I've…it's just the beginning.

CHARACTER: And where's it going?

AUTHOR: What?

CHARACTER: The story. I mean, presumably there is one?

AUTHOR: Of course there is. It's a…it's a…a journey. A journey of which you will be a part of to some degree. Though to what degree I haven't yet decided…but it's getting smaller by the minute.

CHARACTER: So's your play.

AUTHOR: Look, I told you, it's just the beginning. It...it hasn't found its rhythm yet.

CHARACTER: Mmm...well, the play may not have, but you certainly seem to have hit your stride.

AUTHOR: Meaning what?

CHARACTER: Meaning the constant up and down from this table every five minutes. You're like a damn yo-yo. First it's the dog that needs walking, then it's the laundry that needs folding, then it's the sound of some God awful soap opera I can hear blaring from the next room, then it's some uncontrollable urge to dust the mini blinds – it's never ending. Meanwhile, I'm just sitting here not knowing who I am or where the hell I'm going.

AUTHOR: Join the club.

CHARACTER: It's all so static, don't you see? It's completely static. This play is going nowhere fast.

AUTHOR: You can't rush the creative process.

CHARACTER: But give me something, can't you? I need something to work with here. I need to *be* someone. For the love of God, flesh me out a bit!

(*Pause.*)

AUTHOR: The problem is...I'm not sure that I like you anymore. I've a feeling that may be the problem.

CHARACTER: Oh, give me a break, this isn't a popularity contest! *It's a play!* You don't have to like everyone in it. In fact, you shouldn't – it would be boring – which frankly, right now, this is!

AUTHOR: You see, when I first wrote you down, I thought we'd go somewhere together. I didn't know where, but I thought we would. But it doesn't seem to be happening. (*Beat*) Perhaps this just wasn't meant to be?

CHARACTER: Now you just listen to me. I have sat here patiently while you've made every effort to do anything and everything except follow through on what you started. I've stared into space, I've yawned, I've twiddled my thumbs, I've even – in my excruciating boredom – tried very hard to imagine a life for myself out of my own head. But I can't. Only you have the power to do that. So for the love of God, do it!

AUTHOR: I'm sorry...I don't think that I can. I think this may all have been a big mistake. I think, perhaps, I should start again.

CHARACTER: Don't you dare!

AUTHOR: It's not you, really it isn't.

CHARACTER: You just said it was.

AUTHOR: No, it's me, I...I should never have thought of you.

CHARACTER: Well, unless I'm missing something, you hardly have, have you?

AUTHOR: No, not a lot. But just enough, I suppose...to be too much.

CHARACTER: Oh, you *really* know how to make a person feel good? What a charmer. I'd just *love* to sit down and have dinner with you sometime. *Jesus!*

AUTHOR: It's nothing personal.

CHARACTER: I wouldn't know – I was never made a person.

AUTHOR: Well...probably for the best.

CHARACTER: Oooh...you really are a piece of work, aren't you?

AUTHOR: All I meant was–

CHARACTER: I know exactly what you meant, you supercilious, self-important, self-pitying, self-indulgent, self-aggrandizing...self! You think you're so high and mighty, but let me tell you something – one day...one day, when you're lying on some cold, hard park bench, stinking of piss and coughing up snot, I'll be there. I'll be there, and I'll be laughing; laughing *so* hard. Laughing and clapping and dancing and singing and celebrating everything that makes you utterly disgusting yet still cling to life because you don't have the guts to kill yourself.

(*Pause.*)

AUTHOR: And this little tantrum was intended to do what? Change my mind?

CHARACTER: No...just make me feel better.

AUTHOR: Did it?

CHARACTER: Somewhat.

AUTHOR: It doesn't change anything.

CHARACTER: There's precious little to change.

AUTHOR: My mind's made up. I'm sorry it had to be this way.

CHARACTER: Wait! Wait!

AUTHOR: What?

(*Pause.*)

CHARACTER: Just give me another chance. Think about me a bit more. Focus on me a little harder. Maybe...maybe things will start clicking. Maybe you'll find hidden depths to me – sides of me you never imagined were there. And before you know it, I could be kick-starting your imagination into producing something magnificent. Something game-changing. Something that shifts your career – such as it is – to a whole new level.

(*Pause.*)

AUTHOR: I don't think so.

CHARACTER: (*Hissing*) *You don't think so?*

AUTHOR: No. You're just not doing it for me. Let's face it, you're a non-starter.

CHARACTER: *Me! Me! I'm* the non-starter? Oh, you have some nerve, mister, you have *some* nerve. My God, the audacity! I think it's high time you took a long, hard look in the mirror, buddy. Then you'll come face-to-face with the real non-starter around here. You prance around this place like some pretentious dick-on-a-stick, thinking you're *so* artistic, and *so* literary. "Look at me, I'm a writer." "Look at me, I'm a playwright; I'm so *intellectual*; I'm so *esoteric*; a struggling, penniless martyr to my art." "I go forth like Quixote, noble and proud in the face of the doubters and non-believers, and do it all with my head held high and a fountain pen rammed up my precious, tortured ass!"

AUTHOR: You have *no* right to speak to me like that!

CHARACTER: But what do you really do, *really?* Not much

of anything, really. You just like to *think* you do.

AUTHOR: Stop it!

CHARACTER: Because it makes you feel *important*. It makes you feel like you *matter*.

AUTHOR: I said, stop it!

CHARACTER: But guess what? News flash — *ya don't!*

AUTHOR: Enough!

CHARACTER: Hate to break it to ya, buddy — but ya ain't curin' cancer here.

AUTHOR: I'm warning you!

CHARACTER: Hell, you're not even writing a lousy play.

AUTHOR: All right, that's it! This is the end.

CHARACTER: What?

AUTHOR: I refuse to be spoken to like that by someone who *I personally* brought into being.

CHARACTER: You know, for a second there you sounded just like my father.

AUTHOR: You don't have a father. You don't even have a backstory.

CHARACTER: I was pretending.

AUTHOR: In fact…I've decided to make you an orphan.

CHARACTER: No!

AUTHOR: Yes. An orphan. Not only that…an orphan with a deadly and incurable disease.

CHARACTER: So it's a *tragedy. Now* we're getting somewhere.

AUTHOR: One of us is.

CHARACTER: No, please! You said there'd be no violence!

AUTHOR: It'll be painless.

CHARACTER: You bastard!

AUTHOR: (*Solemnly putting pen to paper*) And sadly, after many months of struggle, our tragic orphan's vital organs began to fail.

CHARACTER: No, please!

AUTHOR: It all happened so suddenly – so unexpectedly. There was nothing anyone could do. The doctor turned his head away in resignation.

CHARACTER: Please, no!

AUTHOR: The author looked toward the heavens in search of solace...and perhaps...a little inspiration.

CHARACTER: Please, I beg of you!

AUTHOR: Unable to fight any longer, the poor wretch finally breathed its last breath.

> (*CHARACTER breaths heavily, then slumps forward onto the table. Pause.*)

AUTHOR: And then...the poor devil was gone. Such a short, sad life, truncated – perhaps mercifully – by a ruthless disease and a writer's frustration. (*Beat*) The end.

> (*AUTHOR tears out a page from the pad, screws it into a ball and throws it across the room.*)

AUTHOR: Now what?

> (*As the AUTHOR buries his head in his hands, the lights fade down to BLACK.*)

END OF PLAY

An Honest Mistake

AN HONEST MISTAKE

1M/1F

Madge has long since surrendered herself to the verbal abuse doled out to her by her belligerent husband, Stan. On this particular evening, however, her fears of a rat beneath the floorboards, combined with her absent-mindedness, result in her dishing up Stan not only his evening meal – but also his just deserts!

An Honest Mistake premiered at the American Globe Theatre in New York in 2001.

CHARACTERS

MADGE: Middle-aged housewife. A well-meaning daydreamer. Inured to the abuse from her husband. A little on the heavy side. Late 20s/60s.

STAN: Madge's husband. Bullying and argumentative. Thinks only of himself. A slob. Late 20s/60s.

SETTING & TIME

SETTING: The kitchen of Madge and Stan's home in London.

TIME: Evening. The present.

At Rise: A kitchen in the London home of STAN and MADGE. STAN is sitting at the kitchen table, hunched over a newspaper. MADGE stands upstage by the kitchen counter. The counter is lined with various glass jars of different shapes and sizes filled with a variety of contents, as well as a number of other typical kitchen items. A telephone sits near the end of the counter. MADGE is found opening an envelope. Upon removing a card from inside it, she begins to read its contents, her lips silently mouthing the words as she does so. Upon finishing, she closes the card and holds it to her breast.

MADGE: Ahh…'int that nice?

STAN: (*Irritated.*) Shhh!

MADGE: It was from me sister, Sylvia – the one in Margate.

STAN: (*Belligerently.*) Shut up, I'm tryin' to read the bloody paper!

MADGE: Listen to this, Stan… (*She opens the card again and begins to read aloud.*) She says, "Dear Madge, sorry this is a week late. Got you and Dora mixed up this year – so she got 'ers a week early!" (*Looking up from the card.*) Ha, ha, ha! Imagine!

STAN: Shhh!

MADGE: Never could keep things straight in 'er 'ead, our Sylv. Runs in the family, I s'pose. (*Continuing from the card.*)

"Ope you 'ad a nice birthday, anyway. Lots o' luv, Sylv." (*Looking up from the card.*) Ahh... 'int that nice?

STAN: Shhh!

MADGE: (*Continuing from the card.*) "P.S. Why not come and visit this weekend? I'll buy ya a nice meal – my way of sayin' sorry." (*Looking up from the card.*) Ahh, bless 'er... 'int that nice, Stan?

STAN: 'Ow am I supposed to read this bloody paper with you yakkin' in me ear'ole? Can't you shut that trap for five minutes?

MADGE: Don't you fancy it, then?

STAN: What? Fancy what? What's for dinner?

MADGE: I fancy it. I quite like Margate.

STAN: Margate? What d'ya wanna go to that shit 'ole for? Anyway, I'm not spendin' two days 'oled up with that pinched-faced sister of yours – you know I can't stand 'er. 'Er and that stuck-up 'uband of 'ers, thinkin' they're a cut above the rest of us, just 'cause they got some poxy time-share in the Costa-del-bleedin'-Sol!

MADGE: Pr'aps I could go on me own, then.

STAN: What?

MADGE: Pr'aps I could go on me own.

STAN: You selfish cow! What about me? Who'd do the cookin'? The bleedin' servants, I s'pose?

MADGE: I could make ya sandwiches, and bits and bobs – to tide you over.

STAN: You're the bloody limit, you are, aren't ya? As if it's not bad enough I've 'ad to put up with thirty-odd years of your shitty cookin', bollockin' up me stomach – almost sendin' me to the bleedin' 'ospital – now you wanna starve me to death!

MADGE: But, Stan, I could make– (*Suddenly distracted by something she's heard.*) Listen! There it is again!

STAN: There what is again?

MADGE: That rat. Can't you 'ear it?

STAN: No, I can't 'ear it.

MADGE: Listen! (*Pause.*) It's scratchin'…or gnawin', or summit.

STAN: Oh yeah, I can 'ear it. And I've got summit to say to it, too: where's my bloody dinner?

MADGE: It's a rat, Stan. A rat! They're 'orrible. I don't wanna a rat in me 'ouse, do I?

STAN: I told you before, it's not a rat – it's a mouse. And if that fat, lazy over-fed cat o' yours is too bone idle to kill it, we

71

should 'ave 'em both put down.

MADGE: Don't be like that, Stan. Moxie can't 'elp it. A rat's prob'ly not appealin' to 'er. Everythin' she eats comes out of a tin, dunnit? She's lost the animal instinct, I s'pect.

STAN: Yeah, well most of what I eat comes out of a tin an' all, and I 'aven't lost me animal instinct, 'ave I? – I'm bloody starvin'. What's for dinner?

MADGE: Any'ow, I've taken care of it. Come tomorrow mornin' I s'pect we'll all be sleepin' a bit easier.

STAN: Are you deaf? I asked you what's for dinner?

MADGE: Toad-in-the-'ole.

STAN: Toad-in-the-'ole? We 'ad that last Friday. Gor, bloody 'ell! You've got about as much imagination as a bleedin' minnow, you 'ave, ain't ya?

MADGE: But you never like it when I try somethin' a bit new, Stan. You always say it's muck and I end up goin' down the chippie.

STAN: What d'ya mean? Like that curry crap ya slopped up last week? On the crapper all night with the runs. Is that what you want? You vindictive cow!

> (*STAN reverts back to reading his newspaper. MADGE hypothesizes.*)

MADGE: I followed the recipe. Least, I think I did. Pr'aps it was 'cause it was from an old book. You know, from when they first come 'ere – the Hindus and such. I got it from that second'and bookshop on Moulton Street. Ooh! I forgot to tell ya, din' I? He ran off – Mr. Truelove, the owner – with the cashier. She was only nineteen. They'd been married for twenty-two years – 'im an' 'is wife, that is, not the cashier. Pr'aps I put too much coriander. 'Course, she could'a been married, too, I s'pose. It's anythin' goes, these days, innit? Gawd knows where they are now…Morocco, I s'pose…or Sweden. It was only 50p. 'Course, she may 'ave undercharged me. Well, she's not to know, is she? She's new – or was. S'pect it *was* too much coriander. Well, 'ow you s'posed to know? There's not much call for it, is there? Not in normal food. Imagine 'is poor wife.

STAN: Gor, bloody 'ell! Listen to this… (*Reading from his newspaper.*) "Beer, as in all alcoholic drinks, is made by fermentation caused by bacteria feedin' on the yeast cells, then defecatin'. This bacterial excrement is called alcohol." (*Looking up from his newspaper.*) No wonder me 'ead always feels like shit in the mornin's. I always put it down to the sound of your naggin' voice.

MADGE: Peas or beans?

STAN: What?

MADGE: Peas or beans?

STAN: Peas.

(STAN continues with his newspaper. MADGE moves to the counter to prepare the peas.)

STAN: And what's for afters?

MADGE: No afters today, Stan. I'm ever so sorry.

STAN: "No afters today?" What d'ya mean, "No afters today?" What d'ya think you are, a bleedin' restaurant? Afters are off, are they?

MADGE: Well, I got behind, din' I? *(Enthusiastically.)* You can 'ave a biscuit?

STAN: A biscuit? What am I gonna do with a bloody biscuit, for God's sake?

MADGE: Sorry, Stan, I meant to, but I got behind, din' I?

STAN: Got behind? 'Ow can you get behind? You don't do bugger all. Sittin' 'ere all day watchin' the bloody telly.

MADGE: It's Monday, Stan – I get me 'air done on Mondays.

STAN: You an' your bloody auburn tints. What a waste o' bloody money that is. What if I wanted to get me 'air done, eh? What if I wanted auburn bloody tints? Then where would we be? We'd be in the bloody poor house, that's where we'd be. Dunno what you wanna get yourself all tarted up for, anyway – no one's gonna look at ya.

MADGE: Well, I wouldn't 'ave got behind, only the woman in behind me was eighty. She was eighty – today. And 'er son and 'er daughter-in-law were comin' over to 'elp 'er celebrate. Bringin' over some Chinese, or summit. Any'ow, she said she was behind – not behind me – which she was – but runnin' behind – and I felt ever so sorry, so I let 'er go in front, so then, 'course, I was behind.

STAN: And I get a friggin' biscuit? You thoughtless bint!

MADGE: Sorry, Stan.

STAN: Just get me bleedin' dinner and stop ya bellyachin'. I'm up to 'ere with you.

MADGE: (*Continuing with the dinner preparations.*) Are ya positive you don't fancy Margate, Stan? She's got a lovely place, our Sylv. All mod cons. You'd be ever so comfy. I like seein' the sea once in a while. Just goes on and on, dunnit? No end, an' always movin'. Makes me feel a bit funny. I like it though. She's lucky, our Sylv. Tinned or frozen?

(*STAN is absorbed in his newspaper.*)

MADGE: Tinned or frozen, Stan?

STAN: Tinned.

MADGE: 'Course, I s'pose she's used to it. Prob'ly everyday to 'er. It's all what you get used to, innit? (*Calling off, R.*) Moxie! Din-dins! 'Ope she ain't got lost. Moxie! Mummy's callin'!

STAN: Pen!

MADGE: Who?

STAN: I need a pen!

MADGE: Oh, right – 'ang on.

(*MADGE crosses to the table L. in search of a pen.*)

STAN: I wanna circle this 'orse. Couple a weeks, she'll be ripe for a fiver.

MADGE: (*Returning with a jam jar full of pens.*) Take ya pick.

STAN: What's this, then?

MADGE: Pens. I put 'em all in a jar.

STAN: You and your bloody jam jars!

MADGE: Well, they're all together now, aren't they? Proper. In a…well, in a whatsit. Like an office. Good, innit?

STAN: Why can't ya just chuck 'em away, for God's sake? (*Taking a pen and circling something in his newspaper.*) It's rubbish. They make 'em so you can toss 'em in the bin. But not you – oh, no. You gotta wash it out and stuff some crap in it. This 'ouse is wall-to-bleedin'-wall with jam jars you've stuck some crap into. No wonder it looks like a bleedin' pigsty.

MADGE: Well, it's a waste otherwise, Stan. They're still

good. Rinse 'em out an' you can put allsorts in 'em. "Waste not, want not," my mum always said.

STAN: Your mum – that's a laugh. I s'pose 'er 'ouse was shagged up with a lotta jam jars, too, was it? What a bloody family. Pity she didn't spend more time teachin' you 'ow to cook, instead of 'ow to fill up yer 'ouse with crap. Should've asked my mum – she knew 'ow to cook – she'd 'a taught ya. Then, pr'aps, I wouldn't 'ave to put up with all that pigswill you keep lousin' up me stomach with.

MADGE: Wouldn't cost extra, Stan. Got a bit saved up, see? Not much – few quid, that's all – but enough for the train fare, an' whatnot. (*With a start.*) Ooh! There it is again!

STAN: What?

MADGE: The rat.

STAN: 'Ow many times do I 'ave to tell ya? It's a mouse! Who cares about a poxy mouse? Everyone's got 'em. They're all under the floorboards. It's normal. And as long as it stays out of my way, I couldn't give a rat's ass.

MADGE: (*Continuing with the peas.*) Never mind – it'll be gone come tomorrow. I've been cuttin' the coupons out of the paper, see? Use 'em when I go shoppin'. Every time I save a few pennies, I stick 'em in a jam jar. Soon mounts up, mind. (*Calling off, R.*) Moxie! Where are ya, luv?

STAN: Is it ready yet?

MADGE: Just comin', Stan.

STAN: Strewth! Listen to this... (*Reading from the newspaper.*) "A human sheds about 50 million skin cells every day. In about four years every human sheds 'is or 'er own body weight in skin cells." That's disgustin', that is. Your own body weight – 'ard to believe, innit? Specially in your case. Look at ya. Take you about fifty years, I'd say.

MADGE: (*Placing his food in front of him.*) 'Ere you go then, Stan.

STAN: At bloody last! And where's me sauce?

MADGE: Ooh, I forgot.

> (*MADGE goes to fetch the sauce. STAN takes a first bite of his dinner.*)

STAN: (*After making a noise of utter revulsion.*) Christ-all-bleedin'-mighty! This tastes like shit – even by your standards! 'Ave you been buggerin' about with the recipe again?

MADGE: No, Stan, same as always.

STAN: Well, 'urry up with that sauce! I can't eat this if I don't 'ave summit to smother the taste. This ain't toad-in-the-'ole, it's toad-in-the-shit-'ole!

> (*MADGE hands him the sauce, which STAN proceeds to pour all over the food.*)

MADGE: Ooh, won't I be glad come tomorrow mornin'. Thought of that rat gives me the willies. That's why I put down a bit o' rat poison. Well, someone 'ad to do summit, didn't they? And ya can't blame Moxie – she's too domesticated, 'int she? Wonder if Sylv uses coupons. Prob'ly not. Prob'ly too busy, what with two teens and a golden retriever on 'er plate.

STAN: Gor, bloody 'ell! This is evil, this is! Bloody evil! You've 'it new lows, you 'ave – if that's possible. (*Reaching for the sauce bottle.*) Gimme some more o' that sauce.

MADGE: Same recipe, Stan. Nothin' different. Wonder if Sylv's 'usband likes toad-in-the-'ole. Bit bland for them, I s'pect. S'pect they're more into spicy foods, what with that flat in Spain, an' all. (*Her memory suddenly jogged.*) Ooh, 'ang on, though. There was somethin' a bit different, come to think of it. Struck me funny at the time. What was it?

> (*STAN suddenly begins to convulse, his hands clutching his stomach.*)

MADGE: Oh, I know – it was the jar. Me self-raisin' flour jar. It was smaller than usual. I thought to meself at the time, "That's a bit funny, innit?" I mean, 'ow can a jar get smaller? But I didn't like to dwell on it in case me faculties were goin'. I mean, who wants to dwell on that? So I just put it down to bein' at sixes and sevens. I was runnin' behind, see – 'cause o' that eighty-year-old. Ever so nice, she was. 'Ope she liked 'er Chinese.

> (*STAN begins to retch violently.*)

MADGE: Was a bit small, though – for self-raisin' flour. 'Ere, you don't s'pose I could've… Gawd luv us! I 'ope I didn't get 'em mixed up! I better check.

(*MADGE moves to the kitchen counter to inspect her jars. STAN falls to the floor, writhing in agony.*)

MADGE: 'Ere it is.

(*MADGE holds up the jar to the light and begins to shake its contents. STAN'S groans and movements gradually weaken.*)

MADGE: (*Assuredly.*) No. No, this is definitely not me self-raisin' flour. The jar's much too small, for one thing. And for another, it's not powdery enough. This almost looks like little granules. Whatever is it then? (*A moment of contemplation, then, with great relief.*) Oh, I know what it is, silly! It's me rat poison!

(*STAN lets out a final, painful moan before falling silent.*)

MADGE: So what's 'appened to me self-raisin' flour? I knew I should'a made labels. Got an 'ead like a sieve, I 'ave. Oh well, too late now, Madge. (*She looks around briefly before spotting a larger jar near the end of the counter.*)   Ahh, there it is! (*She picks up the jar of self-raising flour and ponders for a moment, as another suspicion begins to form in her mind.*) But if that's the rat poison in that jar, then that means… (*With an expression of horror she looks over to where STAN had been sitting.*) I put down self-raisin' flour for the rat! (*Clasping her hands to her face.*) Gawd 'elp us, Madge, whatever 'ave you done now? What good's that gonna do? You can't kill a rat with self-raisin' flour, can ya? (*Suddenly not so sure.*) Or can ya? Pr'aps ya can.

Pr'aps it'll self-raise up inside it, or summit, an' explode. Ooh, I 'ope so. Gawd, let's 'ope so. (*Just then the telephone rings. She answers it.*) 'Ello? (*With pure delight.*) 'Ello, Sylv! Fancy you callin' – I was just thinkin' 'bout you... What?... I did, Sylv – came today. Thanks ever so much... What?... Don't be daft, Sylv. Better late than never, that's what I always say... What?... I did and I'd love to. You know 'ow I like Margate, an' it's been ages since I seen the sea. Be smashin', won't it?... Stan? No, I don't think so, luv – 'is stomach again, you know 'ow it is... Yeah, be lovely, won't it? Just like old times... What?... Yeah, I was thinkin' the nine o'clock train, an' all... See ya tomorra' then, luv... What's that?... I told ya, don't be silly, Sylv. It was an 'onest mistake, wannit? We all get in a dither now and then. Runs in our family, I'd say... Yeah, all right then, luv, ta-ta! (*She hangs up the telephone.*) Bless 'er 'eart.

(*The meow of a cat is heard, off R. As MADGE turns and looks, her face lights up with joy.*)

MADGE: Moxie! Ahh, Moxie, there you are. I was gettin' worried about you. Thought pr'aps that rat 'ad got the better of ya. Still, never mind – mummy 'ad a feelin' you'd show up sooner or later.

(*With an expression of blissful happiness, MADGE exits R. to meet MOXIE as the lights fade to BLACK.*)

END OF PLAY

Filler

FILLER

1M/1F

Two characters come to realize that the extended scene written for them in the middle of the play has no intrinsic value, does nothing to propel the story forward, and to all intents and purposes is completely extraneous. Their raison d'être pulled from under them, can they still maintain their credibility and sanity through several pages of what's little more than…filler?

Filler premiered at the Powerhouse Theatre in Independence, Missouri in 2013, followed by a production at The Horse & Stables theatre in London in 2014.

CHARACTERS

SHANE: Tries to convey a macho image, but in truth is nervous and vulnerable. Perhaps a slight Cockney accent. 20s/40s.

TATYANA: Pragmatic, level-headed, but not without heart. Perhaps a slight Eastern European accent. 20s/40s.

SETTING & TIME

SETTING: An ominous and dimly lit stage.

TIME: The present.

At rise: The room is dimly lit. SHANE is seated in a chair, downstage C, holding his head in his hands. TATYANA paces back and forth, upstage. After a while, she stops and appears to peer out of a window, as if looking for something or someone. SHANE turns and observes her.

SHANE: Any sign?

(*Pause.*)

TATYANA: Nothing.

SHANE: (*Rubbing his face in his hands*) Where the fuck is he?

(*Pause.*)

TATYANA: I'm beginning to wonder if they haven't–

SHANE: Shut up! Don't! Don't even think it. We can't afford to.

TATYANA: He was careless. He was stupid. They could have easily–

SHANE: I said, shut it!

(*SHANE covers his face with his face hands again.*)

TATYANA: Yes, yes, bury your head in your hands – in the sand. But when you pull them away, the reality will still be there…waiting for you….for us both.

SHANE: I just need to think, that's all.

TATYANA: About what?

SHANE: About what we do…if he doesn't show up.

TATYANA: What's there to think about? If he doesn't show up…we're dead.

SHANE: *No!*

> (*SHANE leaps from his chair and crosses to TATYANA, grabbing her roughly by the shoulders.*)

SHANE: Listen to me, Tatyana, and listen good! He'll be here. I know he will. Something's happened. Something's screwed up his timing. But he'll be here. I know it. (*Beat*) And if he isn't…if he's…then we'll…change plans.

TATYANA: To what? There are no others. It all depends on him.

SHANE: No it doesn't! We still have options. (*Beat*) I just…

> (*SHANE returns to the chair and rubs his head in hands once more.*)

TATYANA: Look, this is a one-way street. You knew the

risks when you got into this. If you don't have the guts to follow through when things go wrong, then you should never have got involved to begin with. This operation can't afford people like you.

SHANE: Hey, it's not my fault he hasn't shown up. It's no good blaming me.

TATYANA: No one's blaming anyone. But if you can't keep your head in a crisis you shouldn't be in this business.

SHANE: It's keeping my head I'm concerned about. Now, instead of just standing there criticizing, why don't you try and help figure out how we're gonna get out of this mess if he doesn't show up.

TATYANA: He's not showing up.

SHANE: A real optimist, you are, aren't you?

(*Pause.*)

TATYANA: I think I've figured it out.

SHANE: Figured what out?

TATYANA: This. Us. All of this…perpetual waiting.

SHANE: What's to figure out? We're waiting for him to show up, that's all.

TATYANA: But I told you…he's not showing up.

SHANE: Not yet.

TATYANA: He's not showing up because he was never intended to show up. (*Beat*) It's all a set up.

(*Pause.*)

SHANE: What are you talking about?

TATYANA: Us. This. We've been set up.

SHANE: By...by who?

TATYANA: I'll give you one guess.

(*Pause.*)

SHANE: I don't...I've no idea.

(*Pause.*)

TATYANA: The playwright.

SHANE: (*Incredulous*) *What?*

TATYANA: You heard me.

SHANE: But...that's insane.

TATYANA: Is it? Think about it. Think about how neatly the last scene was resolved – how the scene following this one starts from an entirely different plot point.

SHANE: That doesn't mean anything.

TATYANA: No? Then why are we never mentioned again for the rest of the play?

SHANE: That's not true. We are. We are mentioned.

TATYANA: Near the end in a brief aside from a minor character to tie up a loose thread, that's all. The quick disposal of a thin subplot that was never intended to go anywhere in the first place.

SHANE: No...no, you've got it all wrong.

TATYANA: Shane, listen to me, this scene is completely unnecessary to the overall arc of the story. You know it and I know it. It neither propels the play forward nor adds anything of value to the central plot.

SHANE: And you...you really believe this?

TATYANA: I've had my suspicions for some time, but tonight...tonight the final pieces of the puzzle fell into place. You see, I'd often wondered why our characters were brought back from scene three in such a seemingly random and superfluous way. And tonight it hit me.

SHANE: What did?

TATYANA: This entire scene – this completely meaningless waiting game – was added after he'd completed the original script.

SHANE: No!

TATYANA: I'm guessing somewhere around the third or fourth draft.

SHANE: But why? Why on earth would he do that?

TATYANA: Isn't it obvious? It wasn't long enough. He doubtless foresaw problems getting it produced if it didn't stretch to a full evening's entertainment, so he decided to…pad it out.

SHANE: Oh my God! That means…that means that we're…

TATYANA: Yes, Shane. It's time we faced the truth. And the truth is that you and I are little more than…filler.

SHANE: No! (*He begins pacing the stage, highly agitated.*) Jesus Christ, we've gotta do something! We can't just continue on like this!

TATYANA: Do what? We're merely pawns in this web of deceit. We have no say in it.

SHANE: But we have to do *something*. This is ridiculous. We'll be a laughing stock.

TATYANA: I fear it may already be too late.

SHANE: So…what happens now?

TATYANA: What always happens…we wait.

SHANE: I don't know that I can. Not now. Not now that I know.

TATYANA: What choice do you have?

SHANE: But to stay here and just wait – knowing it's all pointless? Knowing we're just killing time because of a poorly structured play?

TATYANA: We've done it countless times before and we'll do it again.

SHANE: But that was before we knew. Oh God, this is…this is torture.

TATYANA: I doubt it's a walk in the park for the audience, either. Let's hope they remain intrigued enough by the mystery of who we're waiting for and don't start putting two and two together.

SHANE: This is unconscionable. How could he get away with it?

TATYANA: It doesn't matter how, the fact is he has. Anyway, it's nothing new – I see it all the time.

SHANE: I should have guessed. Why didn't I see it?

TATYANA: Don't blame yourself.

SHANE: I should have realized the whole concept was suspect. Two people just sitting around waiting for someone who never shows up – I mean, who could possibly find that interesting?

TATYANA: (*Shrugs*) People are strange. Perhaps they read more into it – see it as some sort of...I don't know...metaphor.

SHANE: Well, I don't. I see it as a cheap cop-out from a lazy writer bankrupt of both ideas and principles.

(*Pause.*)

TATYANA: And yet still we wait.

SHANE: Not me. Not for much longer.

TATYANA: You have no choice, Shane. What's written is written. There's nothing to be done.

SHANE: But I...I can't be a party to this. It's a...a waste of people's time.

TATYANA: Relax. They waste much more of it in far more trivial ways. At least with us they have a semi-respectable excuse.

SHANE: Which is what?

TATYANA: "I went to see a play."

(*Pause.*)

SHANE: So we just…wait…until the end?

TATYANA: Yes, Shane. I'm afraid so.

(*Pause.*)

SHANE: Oh, no!

TATYANA: What?

SHANE: Oh, shit!

TATYANA: What is it?

SHANE: I can't…I can't think straight, it's all…all this crap about the playwright and the scene, it's…it's fucked with my head. I don't… (*Beat*) I don't remember.

TATYANA: Don't remember what?

SHANE: How it ends.

TATYANA: Our scene?

SHANE: Yes.

TATYANA: It's nothing to worry about. It ends very simply. (*Beat*) It ends when the light goes out.

SHANE: That's it?

TATYANA: Yes.

SHANE: All that waiting...all that hoping...and it all just ends...just like that?

TATYANA: Yes.

SHANE: So it was all...pointless?

TATYANA: Well...that depends on how you look at it.

SHANE: But we had all that hope – all that expectation. And then it just ends. Unfulfilled.

TATYANA: Not unfulfilled. Unanswered.

SHANE: Isn't that the same thing?

TATYANA: No. One is a dead end. The other is a question mark.

SHANE: You mean a mystery?

TATYANA: In a way.

SHANE: So it...it was all worth, then? Our scene did mean something after all?

TATYANA: In the grand scheme of the play, probably not. We have our turn in the spotlight, eventually the light goes out, and in truth, we're mentioned again but not really remembered.

SHANE: So...so we really are just...filler?

TATYANA: I wouldn't say that. (*Beat*) Now that I look at it, it's really not been that bad. We had our time together, you and me, and on the whole you were pretty good company to share it with. (*Beat*) And anyway, it couldn't go on forever.

SHANE: No.

TATYANA: So, all in all, I'd say it was worth it.

SHANE: Yeah...yeah, I think so, too.

TATYANA: Good. Now give me your hand.

SHANE: Why? This isn't a...does it become a love scene?

TATYANA: No, Shane, mercifully not. But it is the end.

SHANE: It is?

TATYANA: Yes.

SHANE: Are you sure?

TATYANA: My memory's better than yours, remember?

SHANE: Oh, yeah. I'd forgotten.

(*SHANE places his hand in TATYANA'S.*)

TATYANA: Are you ready?

SHANE: For what?

TATYANA: For what comes next.

SHANE: And what's that?

TATYANA: Ah...well, I'm afraid even I don't know the answer to that.

SHANE: Oh. (*Beat*) That's okay.

TATYANA: Trust me?

SHANE: Yes.

(*Pause.*)

TATYANA: Very well, then...our moment's up. Time to go.

(*They both look skyward as the lights slowly fade down to BLACK.*)

END OF PLAY

A Slip of the Tongue

A SLIP OF THE TONGUE

1M/1F

Miss Perkins, tired of the constant innuendos and sexual insinuations of her employer, Mr. Reams, has decided to hand in her notice. On this particular morning, however, Mr. Reams decides to take things one step further. Unfortunately for him, due to Miss Perkins' natural nervous disposition and a telephone that rings at a shockingly high pitch, he soon discovers he's bitten off more than he can chew...or at least, one of them has.

A Slip of the Tongue premiered at New York's Cornelia Street Cafe in a staged reading in 2003, produced by Einstein's Bastard's Theater Company.

CHARACTERS

MISS PERKINS: A secretary. Nervous, apprehensive type. 20s/30s.

MR. REAMS: A solicitor. Lascivious and predatory. Self-important with an insinuating manner. 40s/60s.

SETTING & TIME

SETTING: An office in the solicitors firm of Reams & Ramsbottom.

TIME: Morning. The present.

*At Rise: An office in the solicitors firm of REAMS &
RAMSBOTTOM in London. MISS PERKINS, a rather highly-
strung secretary, sits at a desk typing at a keyboard. Atop the desk are
the usual items one might expect to find: a computer monitor, a
telephone, various trays and stacks of paper, etc. Presently the telephone
rings – a very loud ring – causing MISS PERKINS to almost jump
out of her skin.*

MISS PERKINS: (*With great alarm.*) Arghh! (*She puts her hand
to her chest for a moment in order to catch her breath and calm herself.
Then, brightly.*) Good morning, Reams and Ramsbottom?...
Oh, Shelley – oh, thank 'eavens it's you... You what?... Nah,
nah, I'm all right – 'cept for 'im, o' course... No, not 'im, *'im*
– 'is nibs – Mr. Reams... Yeah, just the same... I know ya
did, Shell, an' I tried that, but it don't make no difference,
does it? 'E's all over me... it's all sex, sex, sex with 'im...
Well, no, not yet, but...well, it's what 'e says all the time,
innit, and the way 'e says it... Yeah, that's right...exactly,
Shell... I know, but what can I say? It's not like 'e's done
anythin' – it's just the way 'e acts, an'... I dunno... Yeah, I
s'pose you're right... Yeah, I'm gonna tell 'im today... I
know, an' I will, but Gawd knows what 'e's gonna say – I'm
the third in four months... I know, you're right, I can't,
'onestly I can't, Shell. I'm on tenter 'ooks 'ere, I am – tenter
'ooks... Exactly, an' what with this phone goin' off like a
bloody fire alarm every five minutes, it's a wonder I've not 'ad
a nervous breakdown... What?... There is no volume thing, I
looked. An' anyway – ooh, look out, I think I can 'ear 'im...

All right, Shell, cheers then.

(*She hangs up the telephone as MR. REAMS enters R.*)

REAMS: Good morning, Miss Perkins. I do so hope that I haven't just blundered in and cut short an important business call?

MISS PERKINS: (*Without thinking.*) Oh no, Mr. Reams, it was just me frie–

REAMS: I'm sorry, my dear, just your what?

MISS PERKINS: (*A little embarrassed.*) Well, it was just me friend Shelley. She was just ringin' to see if I was all right.

REAMS: All right? Is something the matter, Miss Perkins?

MISS PERKINS: Yeah, well no… No, it's just that… Well, I've got a bit of a cough, see, and… well, she was worried.

REAMS: Oh yes, I do see. Shelley was quite right to call you. A bit of a cough, you say? Dear, oh dear, that is cause for concern. The female chest is, without question, a most fragile instrument, and should on no account be left unattended. Of course, ideally, it should be treated gently by the skilled hands of a seasoned professional, and, whilst I can't lay claim to any formalized certification, I can – as luck would have it – boast to having a substantial number of first aid classes under my belt. I would be only too happy, Miss Perkins – in the interests of public health – to give you a quick once over.

MISS PERKINS: No, I, I–

REAMS: Now, if you'd just like to slip off your top?

MISS PERKINS: No! No, thank you, Mr. Reams. That won't be necessary. I took some cough syrup earlier, before I came in. From what it said on the box I should be feeling as right as rain in no time. No time at all.

REAMS: (*Moving closer to her.*) Irrespective, Miss Perkins, when it comes to the upper torso – especially that of the softer sex – one should never tempt fate. Perhaps it might help if I stroked your nipples?

MISS PERKINS: (*Aghast.*) I beg your pardon, Mr. Reams?

REAMS: Hmm?... I said...perhaps it might help if I spoke to Nichols... Young Nichols in personnel? I'm sure he could arrange for you to have the afternoon off. Without financial compensation, of course, your length of tenure at R & R being what it is. But one's health must come first, Miss Perkins, and I will not have it said that I have neglected my own secretary's perky chest.

MISS PERKINS: What did you say?

REAMS: Er...peaky...peaky chest.

MISS PERKINS: You said perky.

REAMS: I believe I said peaky, Miss Perkins.

MISS PERKINS: You didn't – you said perky, not peaky.

REAMS: No, no, Miss Perkins, I said peaky.

MISS PERKINS: It sounded like perky.

REAMS: Miss Peakins, it was perky.

MISS PERKINS: What?

REAMS: I beg your pardon?

MISS PERKINS: I know you said perky.

REAMS: Are you sure, my dear?

MISS PERKINS: Positive.

REAMS: Good heavens, I do so apologize. A slip of the tongue, naturally. I'm afraid as the years advance, Miss Perkins, the rest of me sometimes has a little trouble keeping up. Not every part, of course. There are parts of me that can still keep it up for…well, for as long as circumstances require. The truth is, Miss Perkins, I remain a very potent force when it comes to the ins and outs of Reams and Ramsbottom, as I hope you will have the pleasure of discovering for yourself. I may no longer resemble a young stallion, Miss Perkins, but I can still extend myself in a number of surprising areas…when I see the right openings.

MISS PERKINS: Yes, I… Well, I… I'm sure you can, Mr. Reams. But I shan't be needing the afternoon off, thank you all the same. I need the money, for one thing, and for another...I'm feeling much better now. Back to normal, in fact.

REAMS: Well, I'm certainly relieved to hear it, Miss Perkins. (*With a sudden change of tone.*) Nevertheless, I cannot tolerate members of staff indulging in personal telephone calls during the hours of business. It displays an utter lack of regard for the trust that we have placed in you as one of our employees, and a shocking lack of professionalism.

MISS PERKINS: But I–

REAMS: Furthermore, we here at R & R pride ourselves on presenting valuable employment opportunities for firm-breasted...or, or that is to say, firm-*minded* young people with a desire to give...or rather, to, to, to *get* ahead. You must realize, Miss Perkins, that when someone adopts a Reams and Ramsbottom position we expect them to display to us everything that that position would imply. We expect our staff to bend over backwards and show us just what it is that they have to offer. This is a man's world, Miss Perkins, as I'm sure you will have discovered, which is why we here at R & R have always prided ourselves on our unstinting support and encouragement of female openings. I'd strongly advise you not to squander this golden opportunity.

MISS PERKINS: But, Mr. Reams, I only–

REAMS: When I took you on board several weeks ago, I thought to myself, "What a breath of fresh air: Here at last is a young lady with a determination to make something of herself." You've no idea, Miss Perkins, how many silly, giggly and, quite frankly, tawdry young women have sat in that chair before you, chewing gum and painting their fingernails, their minds more taken with babies and boyfriends than on getting a leg up. But you seemed different. You seemed almost eager to get a leg up. I had high hopes for you, Miss Perkins, very high hopes. Don't disappoint me now. Let me help you get that leg up.

MISS PERKINS: I… Well, I… Yes, Mr. Reams.

REAMS: Now then, what about my report on the Dunsmuir case – have you finished typing it up yet?

MISS PERKINS: I put it on your desk two hours ago.

REAMS: Very good, Miss Perkins, that's much more like it. Now, let me see, this afternoon I have the… (*Looking through his notes.*) Ah yes, the Schaftenliptzen case. My word, that's a bit of a mouthful, isn't it? (*Beat.*) That reminds me, have you had a chance to get a good look inside my briefs yet?

MISS PERKINS: (*Horrified.*) Really, Mr. Reams!

REAMS: What?

MISS PERKINS: Why do you always have to… Why can't you… (*On the verge of tears.*) I just want to… I, I hate it when you always… It's my job, Mr. Reams, I just want to do my job, that's all.

REAMS: And so do I, Miss Perkins! Good heavens, woman,

do try to get a hold of yourself! You're behaving like some hysterical schoolgirl. I placed a number of briefs on the Schaftenliptzen case in a folder and put it on your desk first thing this morning. Now, whilst it goes without saying that I appreciate how preoccupied you've been in dedicating your efforts to the Dunsmuir case, not to mention the ongoing chest updates with your medically vigilant young friend, Shelley, I really must insist, most strenuously, that you find a way to manage your time more productively. The Schaftenliptzen case, as I'm sure I have told you, is of utmost importance – not only to me, but to Reams and Ramsbottom as a whole.

MISS PERKINS: (*Trying to collect herself.*) Yes, Mr. Reams, I'm sorry, it's just... I thought that... Well, I... I'll look through your briefs immediately.

REAMS: I sincerely hope you will, Miss Perkins, because if the rigours of this job are proving to be too much for you, it would be most distressing for me to have to draw our relationship to a close at such a premature juncture.

MISS PERKINS: No, no, Mr. Reams, it's perfectly all right. It's just... I just haven't been... well, what you might say "on an even keel" lately, that's all. Anyway, I'm... I'm feeling more meself now... really I am. I'll, um... I'll get right on it.

REAMS: Very well, Miss Perkins, against my better judgment, I shall allow you to "get right on it." I shall, despite my misgivings, allow you to... how shall I put it... show me your stuff?

MISS PERKINS: And I will, Mr. Reams, I promise I will. Only, I think I ought to mention that, after today–

REAMS: That's what I wanted to hear. Now then, about my briefs. I want you to have a good rummage around inside them – sniff through them – see if you can't come up with something firm, something hard… something that will stand up in the face of the unresponsive and command their attention.

MISS PERKINS: Yes, yes, of course. But I think it's only fair to tell you that–

REAMS: Hard facts – that's what we're after, young lady! I am steadfast in my conviction that within my briefs their lies something so… unwavering, so… rock solid, that even someone as reticent as yourself, Miss Perkins, would find it difficult to remain tight-lipped when confronted by its probing dialectic.

MISS PERKINS: (*Resignedly.*) Yes, Mr. Reams.

> (*Just then the telephone rings. The loudness of the ring, combined with her obvious discomfort, causes MISS PERKINS to elicit a terrified screech.*)

MISS PERKINS: Arghh!

REAMS: Miss Perkins, please! This is a place of business, not a house of horrors. Now, do try to control yourself, and for goodness sake answer that wretched telephone!

MISS PERKINS: Yes, I'm sorry, I'm... I'm sorry. (*As brightly as she can.*) Good morning, Reams and Ramsbottom?...Yes, yes he's right here. One moment please. (*She hands the telephone to REAMS.*) It's for you.

REAMS: Well, who is it?

MISS PERKINS: They didn't say.

(*REAMS rolls his eyes and takes the telephone.*)

REAMS: Gerald Reams speaking... Yes, this is he... Who? (*With an air of disdain.*) Oh, yes, how are you?... No, no I'm afraid I haven't... Well, this is most unexpected, I must say... At what hour?... I see... Well, with all due respect, I cannot express in strong enough terms how inconvenient this is to my schedule... I see... Well, that's that then... Good day to you. (*He hangs up the telephone.*) That was Mrs. Reams. Apparently she will not be dining with me this evening at Le Coq Rouge – a reservation, I might add, that I have greased untold opportunistic palms in order to retain – as she has made, so I am told, alternative arrangements. (*Placing his hand on his brow.*) Oh, my, my, Miss Perkins, what an unfortunate predicament this places me in. I am now suddenly faced with the unenviable prospect of either dining alone at one of our fair city's most exclusive and discriminating restaurants, or returning home to eat a pre-packaged meal that would otherwise have been frozen for all eternity. I suddenly feel as though I'd been...cast adrift.

MISS PERKINS: I'm ever so sorry, Mr. Reams. Still, never mind, there's always a next time, isn't there?

REAMS: Mmm... (*Speculatively.*) I don't suppose... Well, I don't suppose I could entice you, Miss Perkins, into taking a little nibble at Le Coq Rouge?

MISS PERKINS: No, Mr. Reams, you couldn't.

REAMS: Are you quite sure, my dear? You do know that there's many a young underpaid secretary in London that would be willing to compromise themselves in unthinkable ways for the chance of getting a little Le Coq Rouge inside them.

MISS PERKINS: I'm sure there is, Mr. Reams, but I'm afraid I'm... I've... Well, I have a...a prior engagement, you see.

REAMS: But surely you could break it, Miss Perkins? As I told you just now, opportunities should not be squandered.

MISS PERKINS: But I can't, Mr. Reams, honestly I can't.

REAMS: I see. Then I suppose I shall have to return home to an empty house and revitalize a cardboard tray of assorted iced food products. What a pity. (*With an air of tragedy.*) What a great, great pity.

MISS PERKINS: I'm sorry, Mr. Reams.

REAMS: And do you know what makes it *such* a great pity, Miss Perkins?

MISS PERKINS: (*After a moment. Innocently.*) 'Cause you don't like frozen food?

REAMS: No, Miss Perkins, not because I do not like frozen food. Rather, it is because I do so enjoy…eating out.

MISS PERKINS: (*Nervously.*) Yes, I've, I've… I'm… Yes.

REAMS: In fact, I would venture to say that the experience of…eating out…is one of the greatest pleasures afforded the male specie.

MISS REAMS: (*Uncomfortably.*) Mmm.

REAMS: I don't know what it is? Perhaps it is the rarified sensation of warm, tender young flesh sliding up against my tongue? Do you suppose that that could be what it is, Miss Perkins?

MISS PERKINS: (*A little desperate.*) I…suppose so, Mr. Reams.

REAMS: Yes, perhaps it is. Or perhaps it is the overwhelming pleasure of one's mouth gorging itself on the meat of another? Perhaps it is the intoxicating smells filling one's nostrils, the delicious pent up juices suddenly bursting onto one's tongue, running from one's lips in mad abandon? Could that be it, Miss Perkins? Do you think that it could?

MISS PERKINS: (*Almost hysterical.*) I don't know! I don't know!

REAMS: Oh, but I think you do know, Miss Perkins. I think you know precisely what it is that makes me salivate as I stand here before you.

MISS PERKINS: (*Screaming.*) I don't! I don't!

(*REAMS suddenly grabs hold of MISS PERKINS and pulls her up towards him.*)

MISS PERKINS: Mr. Re–

(REAMS locks his lips against hers, thrusting his tongue to-and-fro inside her mouth as he does so, as evidenced by the frequent protrusions from inside MISS PERKINS cheeks. Suddenly the telephone begins ringing loudly, causing an already hysterical MISS PERKINS to scream a terrified, albeit muffled, shriek and to inadvertently bite down on REAMS' tongue. There follows a brief moment of stillness as both attempt to comprehend that which has just occurred. Then both, their eyes wide with disbelief, scream in unison with complete horror, the sound condensed by their still interlocked mouths. Finally MISS PERKINS pulls herself away, as blood begins to pour from the mouth of REAMS. The telephone continues to ring. Almost gagging as she does so, MISS PERKINS reaches her fingers into her mouth and pulls out a surprisingly large portion of REAMS' tongue. REAMS, blood still seeping from his mouth, attempts to ask MISS PERKINS to answer the telephone.)

REAMS: Angha ga hong!

MISS PERKINS: I… I'm sorry…what?

REAMS: Angha ga hong!

MISS PERKINS: I beg your pardon, Mr. Reams…the hong?

REAMS: (*Wildly pointing his finger at the telephone.*) Ga hong! Angha ga hucking kegahong!

MISS PERKINS: Oh… Oh, yes, of course. (*As brightly as possible under the circumstances.*) Good morning, Reams and Ramsbottom?… Oh, oh good morning, Mr. Ramsbottom… Yes… No, I'm afraid he… Well, he…it…it's a little difficult for him to speak at the moment, Mr. Ramsbottom. Things have got a little…well, a little hectic here… Yes… Yes, I'll tell him… Call you immediately… Very important. (*She nods at REAMS as if to underscore the urgency of RAMSBOTTOM'S request.*) Very well, Mr. Ramsbottom… Yes, goodbye. (*She hangs up the telephone.*) That was Mr. Ramsbottom. You're to call him immediately – very important, apparently. (*She suddenly becomes aware of the rather large piece of REAMS' tongue, which she still holds in her left hand.*) Oh, um… Shall I?… Would you like to…?(*Proffering the piece of tongue to REAMS.*) No… No, perhaps not… Well, I'll just, um… Well, I'll just put it down here then…shall I? (*She places the piece of tongue on the desk.*) And don't worry, Mr. Reams, I'm sure, what with modern technology and…well, all that, they can…well…sew it back on, or…or something. (*She picks up one or two personal effects from her desk.*) Well, I'll be off then…Mr. Reams. It's been, um… Well, it's been a…a pleasure working for you and, um… Well, that's that then.

(*MISS PERKINS hurriedly exits L. REAMS stands silent for a moment. As the telephone begins to ring once again, his face begins to contort into an expression of utter hysteria, and a long, loud, guttural scream gradually erupts from within.)*

REAMS: *(In ever-increasing intensity.)* Arghhhhhhhhhhhh!

(His deafening scream abruptly stops as the lights simultaneously BLACKOUT.)

END OF PLAY

The Curious Art of Critique

THE CURIOUS ART OF CRITIQUE

2M/1F

When reaction to his work on a new drama appears tepid at best, the director decides he must tackle the problem head-on and root out whatever it is that's leaving the audience unmoved. One way or another, the evening seems destined to end in tears.

CHARACTERS

ART: The Director. Age open.

JAMES: Receiving notes from the director. 20s/30s.

STEPHANIE: Receiving notes from the director. 20s/30s.

SETTING & TIME

SETTING: A stage.

TIME: The present.

At rise: There is a table downstage C. with three chairs placed around it. In the stage R. chair sits JAMES, and in the stage L. chair sits ART. The chair between them is empty. ART is holding his head in his hands. After a moment he looks up and sighs heavily.

ART: The thing is, Jim…oh, may I call you Jim? I know it's James, but I like to feel that we're… (*Gesturing with his hands to make his point*) Do you know what I mean?

JAMES: Yeah, yeah.

ART: It just makes it more…I don't know…*real.*

JAMES: Sure.

ART: Especially in a little one-on-one like this.

JAMES: Yeah, no problem.

ART: I'm so glad. I'm Arthur, of course, but…to you, Jim…I am *Art.*

JAMES: Yeah, all right, Art – so what's the problem?

ART: Don't you just hate that word…*problem?*

JAMES: No, not really.

ART: No? Oh, I do – *loathe* it. Anyway...the reason I wanted to have this little chat with you, Jim, is because...well, first off, let me say this has absolutely nothing to do with your performance this evening.

JAMES: Okay.

ART: Nothing. Zero. Zip.

JAMES: Well...that's good.

ART: Because what you have to offer is nothing short of...sensational.

JAMES: Really?

ART: Oh, yes. I would describe you as a *major* talent.

JAMES: *Really?*

ART: Quite remarkable.

JAMES: Wow!

ART: Don't sound so surprised. Surely you're aware of the extraordinary gifts you possess?

JAMES: Well, I...you know...I suppose we all like to think we have...*something.*

ART: I'm more inclined to think that you, Jim, have everything...and more besides.

JAMES: Whoa! That's amazing. Can you really tell...I mean...just from what you've seen tonight?

ART: I have been in this business for *many* years, Jim. Many, many years. I've seen it all. But rarely do I ever come across...whatever it is that you have.

JAMES: I'm...I don't know what to say. I'm humbled.

ART: Be humbled, Jim. But not by my words – by your own brilliance.

JAMES: And you could see all that...here tonight.

ART: Oh, yes. I was watching you *very* carefully. *You* specifically.

JAMES: Wow. Good job I didn't know or I'd have probably been, you know...thrown off.

ART: Yes. Which rather brings me to the main reason for this little tête-à-tête.

JAMES: Okay.

ART: You see, it would be remiss of me, regardless of your bountiful talents, if I didn't point out... (*Sighs heavily*) Oh, how do I put this without sounding harsh? (*Beat*) Areas for improvement?

JAMES: Well, yeah, of course. I mean, you're the director.

ART: Yes. Yes, I am, Jim. The success or failure of the entire production rests on my shoulders alone. It is an *immense* responsibility that would *crush* a lesser man. And I do not take it lightly. And for that reason alone, I am forced to return to that most vile of all words...*problem*.

JAMES: Well, if it's not right, you know...you gotta let me know.

ART: Yes. Yes, I must. (*Suddenly stands and clasps his head in his hands*) God, I hate my job sometimes!

JAMES: No, no, it's okay, really. I...I don't mind.

ART: But *I* mind, Jim. *I* mind. It all just seems so ridiculous somehow, don't you think? All this finding fault and criticizing, when all you really want to do is enjoy everything your eyes are bearing witness to...to be swept away in its rapture.

JAMES: Not if there's a fault, no.

ART: Oh, this mad, insane profession! *Why* did I allow it to seduce me?

JAMES: I expect...because you love it, Art.

(*ART sits back down in his chair and regains his composure.*)

ART: Yes. (*Beat*) Yes, I suspect you're right, Jim. It may have taken me by force, but...ever since, I've been smitten – prostrate and yielding to its every whim.

JAMES: Yeah, well, so um...what's the problem?

ART: Ah, yes, the, um...*problem*. Yes, well...uh...perhaps this would be a good time to bring in Stephanie.

JAMES: Stephanie?

ART: Yes. You don't mind, do you?

JAMES: Uh...no, no.

ART: (*Calling off*) Stephanie! Stephanie, dear! I'm ready for you now!

> (*STEPHANIE enters from stage R. looking nervous and confused.*)

ART: There she is! What an angel – and pretty as a picture. Sit down here, my love, next to me.

> (*STEPHANIE sits in the empty chair between ART and JAMES. STEPHANIE and JAMES nod and smile at each other.*)

ART: Stephanie, can I first tell you that you were *magnificent* out there tonight. Dare I use the word...dynamite?

STEPHANIE: Oh...well, thank you. Thanks very much.

ART: I had my eye on you, too, you see? Eyes like a hawk, even with contacts.

STEPHANIE: Well, it's…nice to be noticed…amongst all the rest.

ART: Steph, Steph, who could *not* notice you? You were like a beacon out there. Sailors could sail their ships by that luminous face alone.

STEPHANIE: Ohh…what a lovely thing to say.

ART: What a lovely gift to have.

STEPHANIE: Well, I…I do my best.

ART: Yes. I know you do. (*Tentatively*) But…

STEPHANIE: But?

ART: Well…oh, this is so difficult. Sometimes, as I was telling young Jim here…sometimes your "best" needs… (*Wincing*) A little more.

STEPHANIE: More?

JAMES: You want more?

ART: (*Affecting a cringing expression*) Hate me. Hate me now, please. Get it over with.

STEPHANIE: I don't hate you.

JAMES: No, I don't either. Just tell us what you want us to do.

ART: May I? May I really?

JAMES: Of course.

STEPHANIE: Yeah, don't be silly, just let me know.

ART: Oh, bless you both. However did I end up with two such big-hearted, powerhouse superstars in my theatre? (*In an abrupt change of tone*) Right, Jim, let's start with you.

JAMES: Okay.

ART: This play...it contains humor. Not a lot, I admit. But it's there. And with you...I'm just not seeing it.

JAMES: Well, there's some lines here and there, I suppose, but on the whole it's a bit of a downer.

ART: Yes, yes, but that's because it's what we call a *tra-gi-com-edy*. It's *Chekhovian*. It's where we find the humor amidst the pain. It helps us get through it. It's cathartic. And I don't see the pleasure...in the pain...so I need more pleasure.

JAMES: All right, but–

ART: Smile for me.

JAMES: What?

ART: Give me a smile. The best you've got.

(*JAMES smiles awkwardly.*)

ART: (*Covering his eyes and turning away*) Urgh!

JAMES: It's…well, it's not easy to smile when someone just asks you to. You need a…a reason.

ART: I don't. Never have. But that's beside the point. You, Jim, must *think* of something funny. Dig within yourself. What do you kids laugh at today? Amputees? Poor people? Midgets? Whatever it is, you must *find* the answer within yourself.

JAMES: Uh…um…oh, I don't know. You need to hear a joke to laugh. And there aren't any in this play.

ART: Not jokes, Jim, but *humor*.

JAMES: But…can't you just *think* something's funny? Think it but not show it?

ART: Oh, no, Jim. I need to see a response to the material. I need to know – *to see* – that the meaning of the author's work is hitting its mark. That's my job.

JAMES: All right, well, I'll…I'll try harder to show it. Smile and laugh more…if that's what you want.

ART: It is, Jim – in the right places. And I thank you…from the *bottom* of my showbiz-loving heart.

JAMES: I'll do my best.

ART: You're a star. (In another abrupt change of tone)

Stephanie!

(*STEPHANIE jumps, startled by the sudden and brusque shift of tone and attention.*)

STEPHANIE: Yes!

ART: (*Sighs*) Oh, Stephanie. Steph, Steph, Steph. Just look at you. Who could possibly find fault with you?

STEPHANIE: (*With a bashful giggle*) Oh!

ART: Except me. (*Beat*) You see, the problem is, Steph – and it's a big one – is that this play, despite its moments of levity, is in essence a work of *soul-destroying* tragedy. At its core, it is bleak, desolate, and utterly inconsolable. It has an ugly heart of darkness that is at once an indictment of the human condition and a testament to it. *That* is what I want it to show. *That* is what I want people to feel. Are you with me?

STEPHANIE: Yes.

ART: So why do you give me *nothing?*

STEPHANIE: Nothing?

ART: *Nothing.* When I look at you, it's as if I were watching CSPAN.

STEPHANIE: But, I-I–

ART: Trust me, Steph, *believe* me, I can tell what a truly

loving, feeling, caring person you are deep down inside.

STEPHANIE: Oh, I am, I am!

ART: But all I'm seeing is an ice queen.

STEPHANIE: (*Shocked*) A what?

ART: You heard right. *But*…don't despair…well, do despair, that's the point…*but*, I think I may have a solution for you. I'm sure you're very familiar with the teachings of Constantin Stanislavski.

STEPHANIE: Um–

ART: And of his 'system' and most especially of his introduction of the use of 'emotion memory.' And *that* is what I want from you, Steph. I want you to *feel* the raw pain of what's happening on stage by internally reliving some unspeakable, painful, catastrophic event that occurred in your own life. So, come on – what do you have?

STEPHANIE: Well, I don't know that I want to…I mean…it's a bit personal, really. Don't you think?

ART: *Art*… is personal. There is nothing *more* personal. Now, come along, stop being so coy and precious and tell me something truly, truly horrible that you lived through. We all have one. And I want horrid with a big 'H.'

STEPHANIE: I'm…I'm thinking.

ART: Dig deep, Stephanie. I want real human misery. So what is it? There has to be something. Something that scarred you like nothing else. Something that shut your world down. Something that still tortures you to this very day. The love of your life that dumped you for your best friend? A dearly beloved pet that passed away? A relative gassed in the Holocaust? Anything, something – you have to give me *something*, Stephanie.

STEPHANIE: Well...

ART: Yes?

STEPHANIE: I don't...tell many people about this, but...

ART: Yes, yes?

STEPHANIE: When I was seven-years-old, my mother...committed suicide in front of me. Hanged herself.

ART: (*Ecstatically*) *Yes!*

STEPHANIE: She didn't mean to...in front of me, I mean. I just walked in at the wrong time...just as she was doing it. And there was nothing I could do. I didn't understand what was happening...what I was seeing. It was all weird. I was only seven.

ART: Of course you didn't – of course you were. Oh, this is *pure gold!* Now, just imagine this: Imagine the very last thoughts that were going through her head as she was dangling from that homemade noose, seeing her precious little daughter below her, knowing she'd just emotionally crippled and scarred her for the rest of her life, and there was nothing, absolutely *nothing* she could do about it…it was too late.

STEPHANIE: (*Sobbing*) I know, I know, I think of that.

ART: Such a haunted, tortured death.

STEPHANIE: Yes.

ART: Knowing that her final, grotesque, selfish act would ripple painfully through the life of her simple, innocent young child.

STEPHANIE: (*Crying uncontrollably*) Yes, yes.

ART: Yes, and *that* is what I need to see from you, Stephanie! *That* is emotion! *That* is what I've been searching for. I knew it was there – it just needed someone like me to bring it out.

(*ART stands and beckons the others to do the same.*)

ART: All right, let's get on with the show!

(*JAMES and STEPHANIE stand and move downstage, STEPHANIE still sobbing. ART puts his arms around them both and leads them to the edge of the stage.*)

ART: I don't deserve either of you, I really don't. Now, you go out there, you take your seats again, and you make me proud! Be the best audience you can be!

(JAMES and STEPHANIE step down from the stage and begin walking up the aisle.)

ART: *(Calling after them)* Enjoy the rest of the show! It's all for you! And remember, *feel* it, *live* it! *(Clenching his fists triumphantly)* I love you guys! *(Clasping his hands to his heart)* Every blessed one of you.

(ART turns his back and spreads his arms, forefingers pointed up and out.)

ART: Okay, everybody – intermission over! Act two places please! Now let's make some *magic!*

(As ART snaps his fingers the lights BLACKOUT.)

END OF PLAY

Carbon-Based Life Form
Seeks Similar

CARBON-BASED LIFE FORM SEEKS SIMILAR

1M/1F

Leslie's decided to give love another try, but in a world of shameless self-promotion, pre-packaged personalities, and artificial body parts, can someone still be loved simply for who they are, or do happy endings only exist in massage parlours?

Carbon-Based Life Form Seeks Similar premiered at the American Theatre of Actors, New York, in 2011.

CHARACTERS

MR. LOVEWORTH: The owner of a dating agency. 20s/60s.

LESLIE: A woman looking to date again. 20s/60s.

SETTING & TIME

SETTING: The Happy Endings Dating Agency in London.

TIME: The present.

At rise: MR. LOVEWORTH is found seated behind his desk, scribbling notes in a book. Presently, there is a knock at the door. Upon opening it he discovers LESLIE.

MR. LOVEWORTH: You must be Leslie.

LESLIE: Yes. And you must be Mr. Loveworth.

MR. LOVEWORTH: Right again.

LESLIE: Sorry?

MR. LOVEWORTH: Do come in.

LESLIE: Thank you.

MR. LOVEWORTH: Firstly, let me say welcome to the Happy Endings Dating Agency – where love isn't just a dream, it's a calculated decision.

LESLIE: Thank you.

MR. LOVEWORTH: Do take a seat.

LESLIE: Thanks again.

(They sit.)

LESLIE: You're a little different than I imagined.

MR. LOVEWORTH: How so?

LESLIE: I don't know. Something about your voice – I imagined you taller.

MR. LOVEWORTH: I have a tall voice?

LESLIE: Well, no, I…

MR. LOVEWORTH: So, what brings you to our humble, and some might say, old fashioned little establishment?

LESLIE: Well, I must admit I did try a few of the online agencies first, but it all felt so anonymous and…well, cold, really.

MR. LOVEWORTH: Yes.

LESLIE: I tried placing a few classifieds, too, but that was worse. Some of the people out there, I mean…really.

MR. LOVEWORTH: You don't have to explain to me, Leslie. We here at Happy Endings are quite aware that when it comes to love, there's no substitute for the personal touch.

LESLIE: In fact, I wasn't even sure I wanted to start dating again, because the way things are going nowadays, I began to think, you know…why bother?

MR. LOVEWORTH: What things?

LESLIE: Everything.

MR. LOVEWORTH: Everything?

LESLIE: Yes…absolutely everything.

MR. LOVEWORTH: But that's rather a broad canvas. Could you be a little more specific?

LESLIE: Well…melting glaciers, rising sea levels, wars, jihads, famine, swine flu, the ozone, the Middle East, Paris Hilton, Somali pirates, identity theft, trade deficits, government surveillance…it's endless. And after a while you start to wonder what the point is in trying to make a connection with anyone if it's all going to hell anyway.

MR. LOVEWORTH: What's going to hell?

LESLIE: This. All of it. All of us. It's all going in one direction and it's definitely not up.

MR. LOVEWORTH: Don't you think you're being rather…pessimistic?

LESLIE: It's overwhelming.

MR. LOVEWORTH: But look around – life carries on…just as it always has.

LESLIE: Of course it does…on the surface. It's all a matter of perception. It's all we have.

MR. LOVEWORTH: But if it's all we have, then why worry? If what we perceive is okay, then everything's...okay, yes?

LESLIE: No.

MR. LOVEWORTH: Why not?

LESLIE: Because it's only our perception of reality – not reality.

MR. LOVEWORTH: Some would argue perception is everything.

LESLIE: Oh, if only it were.

MR. LOVEWORTH: So why did you?

LESLIE: Why did I what?

MR. LOVEWORTH: Decide to date again.

LESLIE: Oh. *(Beat)* I don't know, really. I think I just became bored with my reality.

MR. LOVEWORTH: Or your perception of it.

LESLIE: Yes, exactly.

MR. LOVEWORTH: So you're looking for someone else to fill the void inside you.

LESLIE: What void? I never mentioned any void.

MR. LOVEWORTH: No, but to say that you'd become bored with your reality does suggest a certain sense of emptiness – of something missing in your life – wouldn't you agree?

LESLIE: No, it just means I was bored.

MR. LOVEWORTH: I see.

LESLIE: That didn't sound very good, did it?

MR. LOVEWORTH: Frankly, no it didn't.

LESLIE: I'm sorry.

MR. LOVEWORTH: This could potentially be the beginning of an entirely new chapter in your life, Leslie – a journey that could transform and re-imagine your entire concept of what it means to be a human being on planet earth in the twenty-first century. Entering into a new realm of possibilities simply because you were bored may not be the healthiest approach one would wish for.

LESLIE: As I said, I'm sorry. Perhaps stagnant is a better way of putting it. I feel like I've been stagnating recently.

MR. LOVEWORTH: I'm not sure that's much better. Quite possibly worse. Personally, I'd suggest avoiding such terminology when meeting potential suitors.

LESLIE: Why? It's how I feel. I'm just being honest.

143

MR. LOVEWORTH: But honest isn't always good.

LESLIE: Of course it is. Everyone loves honesty.

MR. LOVEWORTH: Everyone loves honesty when it's saying what they want to hear.

LESLIE: Well I wouldn't be interested in dating anyone who didn't respect honesty.

MR. LOVEWORTH: It's not a question of respecting honesty; it's a matter of respecting you.

LESLIE: But you're saying I should be dishonest. What's to respect in that?

MR. LOVEWORTH: I'm not suggesting anything of the kind. I'm simply pointing out that sometimes the truth can benefit from a little...translation.

LESLIE: Into what? I only know English.

MR. LOVEWORTH: Into something more appealing to the recipient of your truth.

LESLIE: Dress it up?

MR. LOVEWORTH: Enhance it.

LESLIE: Lie?

MR. LOVEWORTH: Reinvent.

LESLIE: But the truth is the truth. Once you start messing with it, it ceases to be the truth.

MR. LOVEWORTH: No it doesn't, it simply becomes an updated and improved version of the original – and who doesn't like that?

LESLIE: Look, I am who I am, and people are just going to have to take it or leave it.

MR. LOVEWORTH: Wrong, wrong, wrong, wrong, wrong. That is exactly the wrong way to go about this. That way of thinking is always and without fail going to prevent you from moving from stage one to stage two.

LESLIE: What's stage one and stage two?

MR. LOVEWORTH: Stage one is the first date, where you discover if the chemistry's there. Stage two is everything else.

LESLIE: Well, perhaps I'll meet a man at stage one who feels exactly the same way I do. Someone who'll say, "This is who I am – take it or leave it".

MR. LOVEWORTH: Perhaps you will. But if you do, I can virtually guarantee you'll be mutually repulsed and disgusted by each other's indulgent, self-centric intransigence.

LESLIE: You don't know that. Perhaps we'll both find it refreshing to find someone so secure with themselves.

MR. LOVEWORTH: Impossible. You'll both be so

convinced of your own self-perfection that neither of you will be able to adapt to the other. Remember, two rights always make a wrong.

LESLIE: I think I'm beginning to lose what little enthusiasm I had for this.

MR. LOVEWORTH: Now don't be like that. There's absolutely no reason to lose heart. You just need to pay a little mind to how others perceive you.

LESLIE: Perception versus reality again?

MR. LOVEWORTH: Exactly. So when you meet a prospective partner, you're not going to gesture for him to join you in some fetid pond of stagnation, you're going to invite him to dive with you into an ocean of endless possibilities. *(Beat)* Is it beginning to make sense now?

LESLIE: It's beginning to sound very aquatic.

MR. LOVEWORTH: And why shouldn't it? It's sink or swim out there, and there won't be a lifeguard in sight. The better prepared you are to face the exciting challenges before you, the less likelihood there is of you coming back to me a dripping, sobbing mess.

LESLIE: But what you're asking is for me to pretend to be someone I'm not.

MR. LOVEWORTH: Wrong again.

LESLIE: Yes you are.

MR. LOVEWORTH: Not at all. You see, in order to pretend to be someone you're not, you'd have to know who you are. *(Beat)* Do you?

LESLIE: Well... *(Beat)* Sort of...in a way.

MR. LOVEWORTH: It isn't a guessing game. You can't "sort of" know who you are. You either know it or you don't, and I can tell you quite categorically that the minute you walked through that door, I saw before me someone who had no idea who they were or where they were going. From the look on your face, to your body language, to the way you dress, it's all a mass of confusion and self-doubt stitched together by a few flimsy, half-hearted, and quite frankly, clumsy attempts at individualism.

(Beat.)

LESLIE: Thank you.

MR. LOVEWORTH: That may seem like a rather harsh assessment, but until we get to the root of what's holding you back, you'll never be able to move forward.

LESLIE: Is that really how I come across?

MR. LOVEWORTH: To me – but then I'm a professional.

LESLIE: And to others?

MR. LOVEWORTH: Well, it won't be delineated in such clear terms, but they'll sense it. You can't hide these things – it's in your aura. And while they won't quite be able to put their finger on it, they'll instinctively know that something's off.

LESLIE: But...I don't know how to be anything other than who I am.

MR. LOVEWORTH: And therein lies the problem.

LESLIE: But this is it – this is me.

MR. LOVEWORTH: Ah, we're back to that, are we? Back to the "I am who I am" mantra.

LESLIE: But it's true.

MR. LOVEWORTH: But it's not enough. It's not enough to just *be* in this day and age.

LESLIE: Why ever not?

MR. LOVEWORTH: Ask yourself why you're sitting here before me now, and I think you'll have the answer to your question.

    (Beat.)

LESLIE: Yes...I suppose you've got a point.

MR. LOVEWORTH: Supposition doesn't enter into it. The

fact is you've made absolutely no attempt at a clear brand strategy to market yourself fully and cohesively to the world in which you live, and until you do, any attempt you make at trying to forge a meaningful and genuine relationship with another member of the human race will be doomed to failure.

(Beat.)

LESLIE: And on the other hand?

MR. LOVEWORTH: There is no other hand.

LESLIE: No flipside?

MR. LOVEWORTH: None.

(Beat.)

LESLIE: But why should I have to brand myself? I'm not a product, for heaven's sake.

MR. LOVEWORTH: Well, not a product, no…an entity, perhaps. A commodity, let's say.

LESLIE: I'm not sure I like the sound of all this.

MR. LOVEWORTH: You're on the market, aren't you?

LESLIE: Well…

MR. LOVEWORTH: For a relationship?

LESLIE: Yes, but…

MR. LOVEWORTH: So there you are.

(Beat.)

LESLIE: Can't I just be the brand I am?

MR. LOVEWORTH: What brand? I see no brand. All I see is a hodgepodge of ideas and abstractions sloppily thrown together without any thought or concern about how they appear as a whole. You're a lazy, living grab bag of nothing in particular, cobbled together with neither faith nor conviction.

LESLIE: That's not fair.

MR. LOVEWORTH: It's not nice, is what it is. Not nice for anyone, and certainly not nice for any prospective suitor that may be looming on the horizon.

(Beat.)

LESLIE: I am me, therefore I am truth.

MR. LOVEWORTH: I'm sorry?

LESLIE: I am me, therefore I am truth.

MR. LOVEWORTH: Was that humour?

LESLIE: No.

MR. LOVEWORTH: What then?

LESLIE: It was a statement…and quite profound…in its simplicity…I think.

MR. LOVEWORTH: No it wasn't. It was an awkward, artless attempt at justifying your unwillingness to change. It was also, I might add, completely emblematic of everything that is wrong with your entire methodology.

LESLIE: I wasn't aware I had one.

MR. LOVEWORTH: Or lack thereof.

LESLIE: I thought it had a ring to it.

MR. LOVEWORTH: It had a clang to it. Look, you toss together a couple of tired, half-remembered clichés, shake them up a bit, sheepishly sputter them out and then expect me to be duly impressed. But where was the effort? Where was the trying? It's the same with everything. Your hair, for instance.

LESLIE: What about it?

MR. LOVEWORTH: I'd wager it's the same style now that you had in school.

LESLIE: No, no, it's um…it's, uh… *(Grabbing a piece of her hair)* I keep it a bit shorter…here…just…right here.

MR. LOVEWORTH: And your dress sense.

LESLIE: I think I look all right.

MR. LOVEWORTH: But all right isn't enough. All right equals invisible. Your look is as ill-conceived and slipshod as that embarrassing statement you just blurted out. And it just won't do.

LESLIE: I'm beginning to wonder if this wasn't all a big mistake.

MR. LOVEWORTH: What, the hair or the outfit?

LESLIE: Coming here.

(*Beat.*)

MR. LOVEWORTH: Look, Leslie, I'm only trying to help you achieve your goals, but if I'm to do so, you're going to have to confront some uncomfortable truths. Now, in prehistoric times, things were much more straightforward. You could simply wrap yourself in a pelt, grunt a few times at your heart's desire and live happily ever after. These days things are a little more complicated. Every aspect of your being has to be cultivated and contrived. Nothing can be left to chance. The way you dress, the way you walk, the way you smile, the way you talk, all of it has to be manufactured with absolute precision in order to create the real you – the one that closes the deal. Then and only then will you have become something truly viable in today's fickle and uncertain market.

(*Pause.*)

LESLIE: Can't someone just love me for who I am?

MR. LOVEWORTH: But if you don't know who you are — what's to love?

(Pause.)

LESLIE: The question marks?

MR. LOVEWORTH: Let me put it this way. Let's say I send you out to meet with a very nice gentleman who you find yourself very attracted to, and the next evening you anxiously await his call. He, meanwhile, that very same evening, is enjoying cocktails with friends who are all eager to hear the outcome of his first date, and to whom he relays any one of the following: "She redefined the word dull." "From the way she dressed I assumed she was manic depressive." "Her hair kept reminding me of my grandmother." "She was nice enough, but God, that annoying laugh!" Or perhaps, "In a million years I could never get used to that nose." (Beat) Do you see what I mean?

LESLIE: (Overwhelmed) I...it's...it's all too much. I...can't do it.

MR. LOVEWORTH: Incidentally, your nose — have you considered surgery?

LESLIE: Oh, that's it. That is it! I've had it!

MR. LOVEWORTH: I was only going to suggest a slight–

LESLIE: This is ridiculous! *(Standing)* I'm sorry, I've had enough.

MR. LOVEWORTH: I'm sorry?

LESLIE: I've had enough.

MR. LOVEWORTH: Look, let's not overreact. I'm here to help.

LESLIE: Yes...and you have. You really have.

MR. LOVEWORTH: Good. Now sit down and let's–

LESLIE: I'm leaving.

MR. LOVEWORTH: Now?

LESLIE: I should never have come.

MR. LOVEWORTH: What about love?

LESLIE: I've gone off it.

MR. LOVEWORTH: But you need it. Everyone does.

LESLIE: It's too much trouble.

MR. LOVEWORTH: But your boredom? Your void?

LESLIE: I'll fill it with something else.

MR. LOVEWORTH: A cat?

LESLIE: A catechism. I'll take the vows.

MR. LOVEWORTH: A nun?

LESLIE: I hear a calling.

MR. LOVEWORTH: I hear nothing.

LESLIE: Thanks for everything.

MR. LOVEWORTH: But don't you want—

LESLIE: Goodbye.

(LESLIE exits.)

MR. LOVEWORTH: A happy ending?

(BLACKOUT.)

END OF PLAY

What's the Meta?

WHAT'S THE META?

2 Any Age/Race/Gender Combination

Two written parts wait to be brought to life on stage. One of them, however, is found to be mired in a crisis of self-worth due to the size and quality of their role. The larger, more developed part must then attempt to convince its smaller counterpart of just how necessary they both are to the production that is soon to begin, and of the true and indisputable collaborative nature of theatre.

What's the Meta? premiered at The Lost Playwrights of Western North Carolina, in Hendersonville, North Carolina in 2008.

CHARACTERS

PART 1: A written part in a script.

PART 2: A written part in a script.

SETTING & TIME

SETTING: A stage.

TIME: The present.

At rise: Two PARTS on a stage in tableaux. After a moment, PART 1 emits a deep sigh. PART 2 turns and looks briefly at PART 1 before returning to their original pose. Soon after, PART 1 elicits another deep sigh.

PART 2: (*Looking back again*) Is something wrong?

(*PART 1 shrugs off the question dismissively.*)

PART 2: I asked you a question.

PART 1: I know.

PART 2: Well? What's the matter?

PART 1: You wouldn't understand. Don't worry about it.

PART 2: All right, first of all you have but the most rudimentary knowledge of who I am – *me* – so to assume that I wouldn't understand is presumptuous to say the least, and more than a little condescending. And secondly, I *have* to worry about it because I'm alone out here with you and a show's about to begin, so if there is a problem I freely and openly admit to harbouring a desire to see it resolved as quickly as possible. Okay?

PART 1: Whatever.

PART 2: (*Enraged.*) What? How dare you – *dare you!* – *you*, as thoughtfully transcribed literature, utter that mindless catchall phrase that is the embodiment of total, unmitigated verbal and mental atrophy.

PART 1: It's not my fault. (*Beat*) I'm a victim of circumstance.

PART 2: What circumstance? What's your problem? Stop whinging and just out with it.

PART 1: I'm…I don't have…I lack motivation.

PART 2: That's it?

PART 1: Yes.

PART 2: So what's the big deal? I don't have it either. Most people don't. We just have to force ourselves. Force ourselves to go on.

PART 1: I can't. There's nothing there.

PART 2: I know it feels that way sometimes, but you just have to buck up and press on.

PART 1: Oh yes, it's all right for you, isn't it?

PART 2: What do you mean?

PART 1: Because you're…fleshed out.

PART 2: No I'm not.

PART 1: Compared to me you are. You're multi-dimensional. I'm just a cipher. A convenient device thrown in by the writer to expound upon a certain point of view.

PART 2: But you're relevant. You have relevancy. You're integral to the story.

PART 1: Only in a narrative sense. I don't really belong.

PART 2: Don't be so self-pitying.

PART 1: I'm not, I'm just being honest.

PART 2: Look, a major and completely unexpected plot point hinges upon your sudden appearance in the proceedings. Without you the play wouldn't be turned on its head at the end of act one, leaving the audience breathless and gasping in anticipation – on a good night, at least.

PART 1: That's very kind of you and I know you mean well, but I'm not so underwritten as to be painfully aware of the fact that I'm just a tool. And I can accept that – I can. But not happily.

PART 2: I think you're being a bit hard on yourself, don't you?

PART 1: (*Defensively*) *I'm* not being hard on myself. It was all I was given.

PART 2: Then make the most of it.

PART 1: Oh, right! Say's you. It's all right for you – it's all downhill for you. You get to reveal a multitude of levels and depths as you continue your ninety-minute journey from point A to point B. Your character's arc gradually draws the audience in and endears you to them in ways that initially they would never have dreamt possible, leaving them satisfied and intrigued. Much to their astonishment, this person that they found themselves initially repulsed by turns out to be a complex, and all too human representation of someone that they can empathise and identify with. As they walk out of the main door into the night air they feel buoyed from a sense of having spent an evening and some hard-earned money in a rewarding and enlightening manner…with you.

PART 2: What's wrong with that?

PART 1: Nothing at all. But it wasn't my journey they were taking, it was yours. I was just a plot point.

PART 2: A vital one.

PART 1: In your story.

PART 2: In *the* story.

PART 1: In *your* story. I am a catalyst – nothing more. I have no depth. I have no raison d'etre. I have no inner life. (*Beat*) And I damned well want one and I don't care who knows it!

PART 2: I think you've already started to give yourself one, don't you, the way you're carrying on?

PART 1: Perhaps. Perhaps it's a start. (*Beat*) But I shouldn't have to fight for it, and that's my point.

PART 2: Why not? Anything in this life worth a damn is worth fighting for.

PART 1: Maybe so, but it's so much harder for me, don't you see, because I…I lack–

PART 2: (*Impatiently*) Motivation – yes, yes, yes, I got that part.

PART 1: There's no need to be so testy. It's not my fault I was underwritten.

PART 2: No, but it's not mine either. I didn't ask to be written as a bigger part. I didn't ask to be more absorbing and relevant to the current state of the human condition. You're behaving as if it were some sort of competition.

PART 1: Oh, "absorbing" are we now?

PART 2: (*Uncomfortably*) Well…I'm speaking theoretically, of course. I mean…that's the writer's intention, it's nothing to do with me. I'm not saying that I'm personally absorbing, I'm just reflecting the viewpoint of–

PART 1: Is this pre-show, by the way?

PART 2: What?

PART 1: This.

PART 2: This? No.

PART 1: Then what is it?

PART 2: It's, uh…it's pre-pre-show.

(*Pause.*)

PART 1: What's that?

PART 2: It's sort of like…Off-Off-Broadway.

PART 1: Meaning?

PART 2: Well, it's not there, but it's not quite there either…so it's sort of almost not quite there.

PART 1: Where's there?

PART 2: Somewhere else.

PART 1: Sounds very ephemeral.

PART 2: Yes it is – and that's the beauty of it. And by the way, you're sounding more dimensional by the minute.

PART 1: Oh, thank you. Against type, I might add.

PART 2: Indeed.

PART 1: Come to think of it, I meant to ask you about that earlier – are we characters?

PART 2: (*Astonished*) Us?

PART 1: Yes.

PART 2: No, no, no, of course not. I'm happy to see you become a little more well-rounded but don't get over-inflated at the same time.

PART 1: Then what are we?

PART 2: Words! We're just words. Well, not *just* words. Words are the most important part. But after all, we mustn't get too far ahead of ourselves – we still only exist on paper.

PART 1: Then why are we here?

PART 2: I'm not here.

PART 1: You're not?

PART 2: Of course not.

PART 1: Am I?

PART 2: No.

PART 1: (*Dispirited*) But I…I thought I was a character. Or at the very least…struggling to become one out of what little I am.

PART 2: No, no, no, there you go again – you have it all wrong.

PART 1: Then what am I?

PART 2: (*Implicitly*) Ink on paper.

(*Pause.*)

PART 1: That's all?

PART 2: "*That's all?*" You ingrate! Don't you have the slightest conception of what that means? You *are* the conception, you fool! You are the birth. Without you nothing happens. Without you there is no play. Without you there is no novel, no film, no poem, nor any of their bastard relations. You are the seed – the root of it all.

PART 1: (*Ingenuously*) I don't feel like it.

PART 2: Not you in yourself, necessarily, but in what you represent. You are ink on paper. From quill to laser jet printer, you are and always will be the beginning. Others may mould you and shape you according to their will – for better or worse – but you will always be the font, in every sense of the word. It's what you are.

(*Pause.*)

PART 1: Gosh…I'd never thought about it like that. All of a sudden I…I don't feel so sketched out and plot-convenient. Thank you. Thank you very much.

PART 2: I'm glad. And don't thank me – they weren't my words.

(*Pause.*)

PART 1: So what's next?

PART 2: Pre-show.

PART 1: And that is?

PART 2: When the others take over.

PART 1: Take over what?

PART 2: Us.

PART 1: Which, in strict definition, means?

PART 2: Strictly speaking I wouldn't like to say, but which includes – though is by no means limited to...makeup, gargling, vocal exercises, diarrhoea, frantic last minute line readings, focus, pace, sense memory recall, and stumbling around in the dark trying to find your spot, praying to God that you do before the lights come up and expose you as a co-conspirator in the enormous piece of artifice that you are attempting to lay before a potentially skeptical, though willingly complicit public.

PART 1: Good heavens! (*Beat*) I think I'll just sink back into the paper and relax for a while, if it's all the same to you.

PART 2: Trust me, I'm about to do the same thing.

PART 1: (*Awkwardly*) By the way…well…if you don't mind my asking…are you male or female?

PART 2: Didn't you read the play?

PART 1: (*Somewhat embarrassed*) Yes, but…mostly my bits…skipped the rest. It was a quick read.

PART 2: (*Reprovingly*) Then shame on you. As I told you before, big or small we are all part of a whole and our acknowledgement of that is the only way we can function properly – all working together. If you don't have the last little piece you'll never complete the puzzle.

PART 1: Sorry.

PART 2: Anyway, does it matter?

PART 1: What?

PART 2: My gender?

PART 1: Not to me.

PART 2: So why ask?

PART 1: Well…I was just wondering if you fancied going for a drink – with me.

PART 2: Now?

PART 1: Only if you want to. I'm not trying to…no strings…I just…well, I sort of like you…in a way, and…anyway…

PART 2: As a matter of fact, I would love to – I am, quite literally, dying for a drink. Let's leave them to do what they will – good, bad or just plain incomprehensible.

PART 1: And perhaps afterwards I could show you a bit of my subtext I've been working on.

PART 2: Easy tiger, let's not get carried away. One step at a time.

PART 1: Sorry, I wasn't trying to…(*Gesturing*) Anyway, after you.

PART 2: (*Gesturing*) No, no, I insist – after you. (*Beat*) Did you have somewhere in mind?

PART 1: (*Begins exiting*) No, do you?

PART 2: (*Begins exiting*) No, but I know a nice place on 46th and First.

PART 1: (*Upon exiting*) Sounds like a good place to start.

PART 2: (*Upon exiting*) And end.

(*The lights fade to BLACK.*)

END OF PLAY

An Embarrassing Odour

AN EMBARRASSING ODOUR

1M/1F

Ethel, a frail, widowed pensioner, sits down one evening to tackle her daily crossword puzzle, when suddenly her tranquil world is turned upside down as a burglar breaks into her home believing it to be unoccupied. While Ethel vainly attempts to forge a relationship with the violent delinquent before her, his concerns lie only in getting his hands on her valuables...that and the repugnant smell that fills the room.

An Embarrassing Odour premiered at the Hudson Avenue Theatre in Los Angeles in 2002, produced by the Women's Theatre Company Los Angeles.

CHARACTERS

ETHEL: A widow. Frail and rather timid, with a sweet, innocent disposition. 78-years-old.

THUG: Callous and brutal in manner. Markedly arrogant and self-enamoured. 20s/40s.

SETTING & TIME

SETTING: The living room of Ethel's East London home.

TIME: Night. The present.

At Rise: ETHEL, a frail-looking woman in her late-seventies, sits in an armchair working on a crossword. In front of her is a very large, sturdy, metallic-looking trunk, partially covered by a piece of lace-trimmed decorative fabric. Atop the trunk, facing ETHEL, is a picture frame. To the side of the armchair, R, is a small table holding a lamp, a porcelain ornament of some description, and a cup and saucer.

ETHEL: (*After a yawn.*) Oh, it's no good, Wilf, this one's got me stumped, good an' proper. I dunno if it's 'cause these are gettin' 'arder, or if me brain's gettin' smaller. They say that's what 'appens, don't they? (*Looking over at the picture frame.*) Pr'aps you know, Wilf? You were always a dab 'and with a crossword. (*Reading from the newspaper.*) Thirty-six down: 'The perfect alibi?' – eight letters? (*Looking back at the picture frame.*) No? Well, never mind, Wilf, I s'pect we're both too tired to think straight, don't you? Time I took me achin' bones to bed, I'd say.

(*Just then a loud smashing of glass is heard.*)

ETHEL: (*Petrified.*) Gawd alive, whatever's that? Ooh, Gawd 'elp us! Wilf? (*She grabs the picture frame and holds it close to her.*) Wilf? Summit's 'appenin'! Summit's 'appenin', Wilf, and I dunno what! Oh Gawd, Wilf, I do miss ya! I miss ya ever so much!

(*A figure slowly appears from the darkness at the back of the room. ETHEL turns her head to one side, sensing his presence.*)

ETHEL: (*Her voice shaking.*) Who is it? What d'ya want?

THUG: (*From the darkness.*) Ohhh fuck!

ETHEL: Who's there? Who are ya?

THUG: Oh, fuck me!

ETHEL: Don't 'urt me darlin'! I'm old – I ain't gonna do ya no 'arm!

THUG: You stupid old cow! Why ain't ya got ya bloody lights on?

ETHEL: They are on, darlin'. Got me lamp on, ain't I?

THUG: That piddly fuckin' thing? 'Ow's a professional criminal, the likes o' me, s'posed to know if you're at 'ome or not with that bollocky fuckin' excuse for a light? Might as well 'ave a bleedin' candle goin'.

ETHEL: I can't 'ave lights blazin' all night on a pension, darlin'. It's expensive, the 'letric. Gotta economise, ain't I?

THUG: Gordon-friggin-Bennett, just my bloody luck!

ETHEL: (*Meekly.*) Where are ya then, darlin'? Don't stand back there in the dark, you're makin' me ever so nervous.

(*The THUG moves downstage R, a short distance from*

ETHEL. *He is wearing a stocking mask and carrying a piece of lead piping.*)

ETHEL: (*Tentatively.*) Oh, there you are, darlin'. See, I told ya, I'm ever so old, ain't I? I ain't gonna 'urt ya, now am I?

THUG: (*Raising his hand to cover his nose.*) Gor, bloody 'ell, what an evil stink!

ETHEL: I can't 'elp it, can I? Look at me – I'm seventy-eight.

THUG: Christ, you old people – ya stink, all of ya!

ETHEL: Don't say that, darlin', I can't 'elp it. It's embarrassin', but what can I do – I can't 'elp bein' old, can I?

THUG: Gawd almighty, I got the luck o' the bleedin' devil, I 'ave. You got no idea, 'ave ya? D'ya know 'ow much more complicated my job gets when there's someone 'ome? It's a bloody 'eadache, that's what it is.

ETHEL: I'm ever so sorry, luv.

THUG: Just shut up, will ya? I gotta think, ain't I? (*Suddenly turning his head to one side.*) Gor, bloody 'ell, you don't 'alf pong!

ETHEL: I keep tellin' ya, darlin', I can't 'elp it – I'm seventy-eight.

THUG: I know, I know, now just shut it!

ETHEL: If I was a bit younger I wouldn't 'ave the smell.

Wouldn't 'ave no problem, would I? But I ain't young no more, see? I'm old – I'm ever so old.

THUG: Are you gonna shut that stinkin' gob, or am I gonna 'ave to smack this pipe across that skull o' yours?

ETHEL: (*Terrified.*) Oh, don't 'urt me, luv, please! I wont say nothin' more – promise!

THUG: (*To himself.*) What a bloody mess. All right, what ya gonna do? (*As he eyes her speculatively.*) S'pose I could kill ya right now? Mmm…pr'aps? Could make ya an 'ostage, I s'pose? Nah…who's gonna pay good money for a sack o' stinkin' old bones like you?

(*Pause.*)

ETHEL: (*Attempting to forge a relationship.*) What's your name then, sonny?

THUG: What?

ETHEL: What's your name then?

THUG: I ain't gotta name.

ETHEL: 'Course you gotta name. We all got names. Even thugs an' 'ooligans got names.

THUG: Well I ain't. And as far as you're concerned, I never will. As far as you know I'm just a thug. Just ya common-or-garden, neighbour'ood thug. Gottit?

ETHEL: All right, darlin'. (*Pause.*) What's that you got there on yer 'ead then, Mr. Thug?

THUG: This? What's it look like? It's a bleedin' stockin', innit?

ETHEL: A stockin'? What d'ya wanna stockin' on yer 'ead for? Got allergies, 'ave ya? I got allergies, an' all. Specially come summer – all the pollens, an' that. Me eyes all red an' runnin'. Ooh, it's wicked, it is. Makes my life misery.

THUG: Look, just shut yer jabberin', will ya? There's only one thing I'm allergic to right now, an' that's smelly old people that can't keep their trap shut!

ETHEL: Sorry, Mr. Thug.

(*Pause.*)

THUG: Got free reign, see, in an empty 'ouse. Do what I want. This 'as buggered it right up, this 'as. (*Beat.*) Oh well, I s'pose I'm just gonna 'ave to take what I can an' 'ope for the best. But I'm gonna tell you summit right now, you fuckin' old cesspit, and you better listen good an' 'ard: You go tellin' Old Bill one tiniest little detail 'bout me – me 'eight, sound o' me voice, anythin' – an' I'll be back. I'll be back an' I'll find you, an' I'll make you wish you'd never been born. I'll beat you so 'ard. I'll beat you black an' blue. I'll smash every single brittle bone in that stinkin' carcass o' yours. You'll be so messed up, your own family wont even recognize ya – that's if ya got any left. You gottit?

ETHEL: (*Shaking.*) Oh, yes, Mr. Thug, I promise I wont say nothin' to no one!

THUG: All right then. So where are they?

ETHEL: Where's what?

THUG: Ya goodies?

ETHEL: What goodies?

THUG: Ya goodies…ya valuables…ya cash?

ETHEL: I ain't got no goodies.

THUG: Come on! Even a lonely, smelly old bitch like you must 'ave a bit stashed away somewhere.

ETHEL: I ain't, Mr. Thug, 'onest. All I got's what ya see. Since Wilf passed on it's all I can do to make ends meet. Don't get much on a pension, see? No room for savin's on my budget.

THUG: Now don't you start gettin' difficult. 'Cause if you start gettin' difficult, then I 'ave to start gettin' difficult. And I don't s'pect you fancy 'avin yer 'ead cracked open like an egg, do ya?

ETHEL: Ooh no, Mr. Thug, I certainly don't! Oh please, Mr. Thug, don't let ya criminal tendencies get the better of ya. I'm ever so old, I am. I'm seventy-eight.

THUG: Yeah, ya smell seventy-eight an' all. Now, I'm gonna ask ya one more time where your stash is, and then you're gonna tell me. And I don't wanna 'ear no "I ain't got nothin' ", 'cause that's bollocks! Everyone's gotta bit a summit stashed away somewhere. See, when I'm on me own I can rummage around to me 'earts content – and sooner or later I'll find it. I always do. Bet you'd be surprised what some o' your neighbours got tucked away in little corners. Very surprised indeed. It's amazin' what ya learn about people in this game.

ETHEL: Done a lot o' places round 'ere, 'ave ya?

THUG: I done a few.

ETHEL: (*A sudden realization.*) 'Ere, 'ang on, I think I read about you in the paper the other day, din' I? You're that burglar they keep goin' about, ain't ya?

THUG: (*Somewhat flattered.*) Yeah, that's me. Bit of a celeb round 'ere, I am. You should be 'onoured.

ETHEL: Ooh, I am. Fancy that. I never met anyone I read about in the paper before. They call ya summit, don't they, in the papers? What is it… 'The Daffodil,' is it?

THUG: (*Angrily.*) Narcissus!

ETHEL: Narcissus, that's it! (*Beat.*) 'Ere, that's a funny name for a sinister, underworld-type like ya'self, innit? What'd they go and call ya that for then?

THUG: (*A little embarrassed. Sarcastically.*) 'Ow the 'ell should I know? Prob'ly 'cause I'm so pretty, ain't I?

ETHEL: Oh yes, Mr. Thug, I'm sure you're ever so 'andsome – just 'ard to tell underneath your allergy stockin', innit? (*Beat.*) This your patch then, is it?

THUG: Yeah. Well, now it is, anyway. Used to be a mate o' mine's, but 'e disappeared. 'Ad gangland connections, see? Least, that's my opinion. Anyway, all that matters is 'e's gone an' now it's mine.

ETHEL: That's right, we did 'ave another string o' burglaries an' whatnot round 'ere, not four months back. An' 'e was a mate o' yours, was 'e? Gawd blimey, what a small world, innit?

THUG: Well, pr'aps not a mate – more of a competitor, ya could say. But I'm in charge now, see? An' I've come to claim me booty. So, I'll ask ya one last time – where is it?

ETHEL: Oh, not back to that, Mr. Thug. I told ya, we're poor. We've always been poor. You can 'it me all ya want, but it wont change the fact I'm poor. Wilf an' I never 'ad much. Spent most of our lives just tryin' to keep our 'eads above water. We were 'appy enough, don't get me wrong, but we never 'ad much.

THUG: (*Menacingly.*) You're not gonna tell me, are ya?

ETHEL: (*Pleading.*) But I 'ave told ya – 'onest I 'ave!

(The THUG moves closer to ETHEL, as she cowers in fear.)

THUG: *(Pointing to the picture frame.)* Who's that then? That's "Wilf" is it?

ETHEL: *(Fondly.)* Yeah, that's my Wilf, bless 'im – back in 'is Merchant Navy days.

THUG: *(As he picks up the picture and briefly studies it.)* Ahh, that's nice, that is. That's really nice. Really touchin'.

(The THUG suddenly throws the picture frame onto the trunk and slams his lead pipe into it, smashing it to pieces.)

ETHEL: *(Horrified.)* Wilf! *(She picks up what's left of the picture frame.)* Oh, Wilf! Me poor old Wilf!

(ETHEL begins to cry as she holds the remnants of the frame close to her.)

THUG: Now then…let's see if that's jogged yer memory?

ETHEL: *(Through her sobs.)* What d'ya wanna go an' do that for? Wilf never 'urt no one. Wouldn't 'urt a fly would my Wilf.

THUG: Times up, old crone. If I stand 'ere much longer your stink's gonna do me in, an' if you keep me waitin' any longer I'm gonna do you in. So ya see, one of us is gonna 'ave to win – an' that means you gotta lose.

ETHEL: I can't tell ya nothin' but the truth, can I? We don't 'ave nothin'. We never 'ad nothin'. 'Ow could we on what poor Wilf made, poor bugger. What 'e brought in paid the rent an' fed us, an' that was about all. Only thing o' value I ever 'ad was Wilf. (*Beat.*) That an' a couple a bits o' jewelry 'e bought me soon as we was married. Only cheap stuff, really, but it meant a lot to us – to me.

THUG: At bloody last! Took you long enough, dinnit? Right then, where is it?

ETHEL: What?

THUG: Ya booty, ya precious little jewels?

ETHEL: Oh Gawd, Mr. Thug, 'ow should I know? I can't 'ardly remember where I put down me glasses from one minute to the next. 'Ow d'ya s'pect me to remember where I put a couple a bits o' jewelry I got donkey's years ago?

(*The THUG stares at ETHEL for a moment.*)

THUG: Now, you could be tryin' to act the innocent, couldn't ya? But call me an old softy, Mrs. Stink-bag, but for some daft, sentimental reason I believe ya. Pr'aps it's 'cause I 'onestly think you're as stupid as ya look. But don't you go worryin' ya smelly little 'ead, 'cause I think I can 'elp ya. See, I'm a bit of a pirate, me. I'm well-accustomed to sniffin' out other people's little treasures, wherever they're 'idden. And summit tells me – I dunno, call it...call it a naggin' suspicion – but summit tells me your booty's 'idden in that trunk.

ETHEL: (*Uneasily.*) Ooh, no... Ooh, no, you don't wanna go

in there, Mr. Thug, there's nothin' in there. Nothin' you'd want.

THUG: (*Slamming the lead pipe down onto the trunk.*) X marks the spot, old crone! Now let's 'ave a look! (He *tugs away the lace-trimmed fabric with the lead pipe and crouches in front of the trunk and attempts to open it.*) What you got this big padlock on 'ere for then, eh? Not tryin' to 'ide summit, are ya? (*He grins victoriously.*) Give us the key!

ETHEL: No, Mr. Thug, please. There's nothin' in there you want.

THUG: (*Brandishing the lead pipe.*) Gimme the key now or I start whackin' – you and the trunk!

ETHEL: (*Reluctantly.*) All right, 'ere it is!

> (*ETHEL lifts a slender silver chain from around her neck, which has a small key attached to it. The THUG immediately snatches the key away, snapping the chain from her neck in the process.*)

ETHEL: Ow! Ooh, careful, that 'urt!

THUG: Shut up!

> (*The THUG attempts to open the lock, but without success.*)

ETHEL: Ain't gonna be easy, Mr. Thug. That lock's old, an' they made everythin' sturdy back then, in my day. Except people, o' course.

THUG: (*Becoming frustrated.*) Come on, ya fucker!

ETHEL: (*Indicating the lead pipe.*) 'Ere, let me 'old yer whatsit for ya.

> (*The THUG instinctively hands ETHEL the lead pipe and continues his struggle with the lock. Finally his efforts pay off and the lock opens.*)

THUG: Bingo! (*Sneering at ETHEL.*) All right, me 'earties, I think it's time for a treasure 'unt!

> (*The THUG lifts open the trunk and looks inside, only to be confronted by a most horrifying sight and stench.*)

THUG: (*In a dreadful cry.*) Oh my God!

> (*ETHEL stands above him, wielding the lead pipe, and lands a cracking blow to the back of the THUG'S head, who slumps forward into the trunk. ETHEL sits back down into the armchair to collect herself.*)

ETHEL: Ooh! (*She drops the lead pipe and tries to catch her breath.*) Ooh! Gawd alive! That almost did me in, that did, Wilf. I just ain't got the strength I used to. (*Leaning forward to examine the results of her efforts.*) Oh, Wilf, I don't 'alf miss ya. You should be 'ere doin' this, not me. This ain't a woman's work, now is it? (*She begins to lift the rest of the THUG'S body into the trunk.*) 'Ere ya go then, Mr. Thug. 'Ere's ya mate – 'e'll keep ya company. (*As she pushes the THUG'S feet into the trunk.*) Gonna be a bit of a tight squeeze, I'm afraid. Still, you'll manage – not as if you're strangers, is it? Mr. Lout, 'ere's ya friend, Mr.

Thug. (*She closes the lid of the trunk and sits back in the armchair.*) Oof! Crime everywhere these days. Dunno what this world's comin' to, I don't 'onest. Now I got two of 'em 'ere. Smell'll be twice as bad. Gawd, whatever shall I do? Well, I'll 'ave to do summit before summer, wont I? All that 'eat – the smell'll be overwhelmin'. The neighbours'll be up in arms. They'll say I can't take care o' meself. But I can't 'elp it, can I? I'm old. I'm seventy-eight. 'Ow can I lift a big 'eavy trunk like that? If I was a few years younger... (*A sudden thought.*) Ooh, I know...pr'aps I can ask Trevor's boy to 'elp me. 'E's ever such a nice young lad. Strong, an' all. 'E can 'elp me take it out back. We can dig an 'ole an' bury it. (*Talking to the trunk.*) Now, don't you go knockin' an' tappin' all night, Mr. Thug, like the other one. It's 'ard enough as it is, tryin' to get a good night's sleep at my age, without all that. Anyway, not much air in there now – don't s'pect it'll take too long. Beats me 'ow the smell gets out in the first place. S'posed to seal up proper, this is – nice an' tight. S'posed to go down with the ship. Wilf got it when 'e was in the Merchant Navy, didn't ya Wilf? (*She picks up the broken picture frame.*) Oh, Wilf! Whatever 'ave they done to ya? (*Shaking off the broken glass.*) Never mind, Wilf, I'll buy ya a new frame tomorrow. Nice an' new. You'll look lovely in it. Better than ever, you'll see. (*A sudden realization.*) Wait a minute...o' course! Wilf! Gawd luv us, o' course! That's it! Where'd I put it? (*She searches for a moment or two before finding what she was looking for – her crossword puzzle.*) 'Ere we are. (*She counts the squares.*) Ha, ha! I knew it! "The perfect alibi?" – airtight! (*Taking up her pen, she fills in the blank squares.*) Innit funny 'ow it suddenly comes to ya? That's the thing about crosswords, Wilf, innit? Take a little break an' go back an' all sorts of ideas'll pop into yer 'ead. (*As she triumphantly finishes writing in the answer.*) Airtight! There we are! (*Laying the crossword*

189

puzzle back down on the table.) Ooh, what a relief that is. Pr'aps I will 'ave a good night's sleep tonight, after all.

(*The lights fade to BLACK.*)

END OF PLAY

A Rebel Among the Wretched

A REBEL AMONG THE WRETCHED

1M/2F

A celebrated, multi-award winning dysfunctional family drama continues to enthrall audiences night after night. But what happens when one of the characters finally decides they've had enough doom and despair and resolves to leave the play to join…a musical?

A Rebel Among the Wretched premiered at The Actors Workout Studio in Los Angeles in 2014. The play was a Heideman Award Finalist in The National Ten-Minute Play Contest at the Actors Theatre of Louisville in 2011.

CHARACTERS

MOTHER: The mother. 50s/60s.

MARGARET: The daughter. 20s/40s.

BILLY: The son. 20s/40s.

SETTING & TIME

SETTING: An impoverished and godforsaken bare stage.

TIME: The present.

At rise: MOTHER *is sitting in an armchair, stage C. She appears to be asleep. After a few moments, however, she suddenly raises her head and yells at the top of her voice.*

MOTHER: *Margaret!*

    (*Pause.*)

MOTHER: *Margaret!*

    (*Pause.*)

MOTHER: *Marrr-greeeet!*

    (*MARGARET enters hurriedly from stage* R.)

MARGARET: Yes, Mother, what is it?

MOTHER: What the hell took ya so damn long?

MARGARET: I'm…I'm sorry, Mother. I came as quick as I could. I was washing ya bed sheets downstairs.

MOTHER: *Bed* sheets? What d'ya mean *bed* sheets? What other kinda sheets are there, idiot?

MARGARET: Well, I…anyway…it's hard to hear with all the noise of the machines an' the water an' what-not.

MOTHER: Stop ya blatherin' girl. I don't wanna hear ya problems or excuses – they're always the same.

MARGARET: But it's the truth, Mother. Them machines are old an' they make such a noise ya can hardly hear yourself think.

MOTHER: Well, I can't see as how that would cause ya too much of an inconvenience. Not like there's much goin' on up there to begin with, is there?

MARGARET: (*Defensively*) Yes. Yes, there is, Mother. I've a good mind, I know I do. I just…never had the opportunity, that's all.

MOTHER: For what?

MARGARET: An education. A proper education. Ever since ya problems started, I've had to–

MOTHER: Oh, so now I'm the reason ya stupid?

MARGARET: No, it's not…I'm not saying that, of course not. It's just…if I'd had the chance, I think I could've…well…I think I could've done quite well.

MOTHER: Ya got no skills, girl – 'cept lookin after me – an the sooner off ya realize that, the better off we'll all be.

MARGARET: I know I'm not stupid, Mother. I know I'm not. I don't have no certificates or fancy embossed papers sayin otherwise, but I know I'm not stupid.

MOTHER: Well…as long as you believe it, honey, I guess that's all that matters. Now, if ya wouldn't mind switchin them thoughts in that tiny little mind o' yours to start thinkin 'bout me for just a second or two here, I'd greatly appreciate it. (*Beat*) For Christ's sake, I'm the one dyin here!

MARGARET: I'm sorry, Mother. I-I got a bit carried away, I guess. What is it ya need? Is it a drink? Ya want me to fix ya another drink?

MOTHER: *No! No*, I don't want another damn drink! Is that what you want? Ya wanna poison ma liver an' keep pushin me a little closer to the grave? Is that it?

MARGARET: No, Mother, I–

MOTHER: When I wanna 'nother damn drink you'll damn well know it!

MARGARET: Of course, Mother. (*Beat*) Is it ya pills, maybe? Can I fetch ya pills for ya?

MOTHER: Oh yeah, you'd just love that, wouldn't ya? Fetch Mama some more pills so ya can knock her out for another couple of hours. (*Beat*) Well, guess what? It ain't gonna happen this time, sweetheart.

MARGARET: Mother, all I was trying to do was–

MOTHER: *Don't* tell me what you was tryin to do! I know all your little schemin' ways an' tricks, an' don't ever think I don't. (*Beat*) Thing of it is, though…none of it matters no

197

more. (*Beat*) 'Cause I want out.

MARGARET: Out?

MOTHER: You heard right, missy – *out!*

MARGARET: You...ya wanna go outside for a bit? Ya wanna get some air? (*Gesturing to help her*) If ya grab your stick an' put your arm 'round ma shoulders, I'm sure maybe we can–

MOTHER: Get away from me, girl!

MARGARET: But I...I thought ya–

MOTHER: I don't mean outta this *house!* I mean outta this god-damned, lousy, miserable *play!*

MARGARET: (*Aghast*) Mother! How...how can you say such a thing?

MOTHER: 'Cause I gotta mouth an' I can make it say stuff, that's how. An' I've had it! I'm up to here with it. An' I want out!

MARGARET: You don't mean this, Mother, I know ya don't. You're just tired is all.

MOTHER: Ya got that right – tired o' this miserable, stinkin family. Tired of all its damn problems. Tired of sittin in this chair night after night spittin ma bile an' bitterness at anyone in sight.

MARGARET: But…but ya can't just up an' leave, Mother. You're the center of the family. What on earth would we all do with you gone?

MOTHER: Well, I guess you an' all the rest o' this sorry, messed up clan are gonna have to start figurin stuff out for yourselves, aren't ya?

MARGARET: I-I just don't understand. What's brought all this on so sudden?

MOTHER: Ain't nothin sudden about it. Been a *long* time comin. I guess I just reached that point where enough's enough.

MARGARET: Are ya…are ya not happy here, Mother?

MOTHER: Well, now…why don't ya just reflect a while on that there question ya just posed to me, young Margaret, an' I've a feelin you'll have your answer in no time at all…bein so smart an' all.

MARGARET: I know it ain't all fun an' games, but we–

MOTHER: No, it ain't! It's nothin but a bunch of unfulfilled lives simmerin with resentment, day in an' day out. An' that's what I want – out!

MARGARET: But why now?

MOTHER: While I still got some life in me, that's why now. I'm old, alcoholic, addicted to prescription drugs, an' this soul-destroyin, downer of a play's suckin the life outta me!

MARGARET: But where would ya go? What would ya do?

MOTHER: I'll find my self somethin better, that's what. A musical, maybe. Somethin where everyone's singin an' dancing an' havin a good time of it.

MARGARET: A…a musical? But that's fluff, Mother. It ain't nothin. Why would ya wanna be in somethin like that?

MOTHER: So I could enjoy myself, stupid. So I wouldn't have to sit around here starin at your long, loveless face six nights a week, plus matinees.

MARGARET: But surely you're too…

MOTHER: Too what? *Old?*

MARGARET: Well, ya ain't exactly–

MOTHER: Don't you worry that tiny little mind o' yours about that, my girl. Still plenty of old croaks out there makin the rounds.

> (*Just at that moment, BILLY enters from stage L. MARGARET gasps in shock.*)

MARGARET: Billy!

BILLY: Hello, Margaret.

MARGARET: What on earth? Ya…ya came back!

BILLY: Yes, I did. It's been a long time.

MOTHER: Well, well…if it ain't the prodigal son makin his return to the family rats nest…right on cue.

BILLY: It's very nice to see you, too, Mother.

MOTHER: Let me guess. Ya been livin in some fancy city somewhere, workin an' strugglin' ya way up until ya finally made somethin of yourself. Only trouble is, ya still can't get the dirt out from between ya toes, nor the poison in the pit of ya soul, so ya came back here to try an' get it all cleaned up. Close?

BILLY: I may have changed in some ways, Mother, but clearly you haven't. You're exactly the same.

MOTHER: Not for long.

MARGARET: Billy, oh, Billy! Ya come back just in time. Somethin awful's goin down.

BILLY: What?

MARGARET: It's Mother – she's leavin.

BILLY: Leaving?

MARGARET: She wants outta the play!

BILLY: Mother! Mother, you can't do that.

MOTHER: Who the hell are you to tell me what I can and can't do? Ya come waltzin' in here after all these years in ya fancy clothes, with ya fancy manners, thinkin you're somethin better than the rest of us. Well, ya ain't! Ya trash. Ya always were an' ya always will be. Trash in a fancy suit's still trash, an' I'm done with the lot o' ya!

BILLY: But...but you can't. You mustn't. I have a whole host of unresolved problems to work through before the end of the play.

MOTHER: Too bad.

BILLY: But...but what about my issues?

MOTHER: Stick em up ya–

MARGARET: Mother! (*Beat*) Mother, would ya please just think again? Think about what you'd be doin to the family – to a respected work of drama.

MOTHER: I'm done thinkin. I'm goin.

BILLY: But you've got nowhere to go.

MARGARET: She's talkin 'bout joinin a musical.

BILLY: You're not serious?

MARGARET: Says she wants to sing an' dance.

BILLY: Margaret, we have to do something – call someone. This is far more serious than I thought.

MOTHER: What's wrong with a goddamned musical? Don't you people ever smile, for Christ's sake?

BILLY: Mother, it's cheap, frivolous nonsense. It's lowbrow spectacle that panders shamelessly to the masses. *This* is a multi-award winning family drama that's been translated into seventeen languages and was hailed by the New York Times as "Harrowing, ground-breaking, and absolutely unmissable." Stars still line up to play the leads, and it's been on every critic's "best of" list since its debut. Why would you give all of that up for some silly, clichéd, theatrical by-product?

MOTHER: Because it's *fun*, ya lifeless duds! Because it ain't some big, ugly, self-pityin, slice o' shitty life. By God, it was a humorless day I shat the two o' ya out from in me, an' ya been nothin but humorless ever since.

MARGARET: But Mother, what we do is important. It touches people.

BILLY: She's right. A work like this connects with people. It helps them realize that their own families – ones they'd always secretly considered to be dysfunctional, but tried very hard to pretend otherwise – are actually completely normal, because in reality everyone's family is dysfunctional to some degree. Which ironically, and sadly for drama, makes the genre something of a redundancy. (*Beat*) Though I've a feeling I may have just undermined my own argument.

MOTHER: Look at ya – both o' ya – you're pathetic! You're both so stuck on some fancy idea 'bout the weight of what ya do that you've forgotten to have a good time. Well, old as I am, I ain't. (*Beat*) But…I will say this before I go. There's one thing this godforsaken piece o' crap's taught me. Somethin, now I think of it, that *is* pretty damn life-changin.

BILLY: I knew it.

MARGARET: What is it, Mother?

MOTHER: All them years ago, when ya Pa just up an' left me, right after he'd seeded me with a couple o' brain-dead tit-suckers that made my life feel so much worse than it already was…well, I just plain hated him. I wanted him to die. But I realize now that he was right. Despite all the pain an' bitterness he caused me over the years, I can see now that he did what he had to. He was right to get out – to leave while he still could. He could tell what a big slab o' misery we were dumpin on the world, an' he wanted nothin more to do with it. And now – slow on the uptake as I am – neither do I.

> (*MOTHER takes her cane and begins to pull herself up from her chair.*)

BILLY: Where are you going?

MOTHER: Ain't decided yet. 'Wicked' maybe. 'A Little Night Music' if the timings right. 'Drivin Miss Daisy' if there's one on somewhere. Not a musical, true, but still a dream vacation from this cesspit.

MARGARET: Mother, don't leave us, *please!*

MOTHER: Sorry, honey. I feel a song comin on.

BILLY: Mother, I forbid you!

MOTHER: Ya do, do ya? Well ain't that nice.

(*MOTHER begins to exit stage L.*)

MARGARET: Mother, *please!*

BILLY: Stop, Mother – stop!

MOTHER: Oh, it's stoppin. It's stoppin right now. The minute I walk off this stage, this whole sad, sorry excuse for a play ceases to be. Without me...ya got nothin.

MARGARET AND BILLY: (*In unison*) *STOP!*

(*As MOTHER slowly exits, perhaps whistling a show tune, MARGARET and BILLY look at each other in disbelief, frozen in tableau, as the lights fade down to BLACK.*)

END OF PLAY

Cocktail Conversation

COCKTAIL CONVERSATION

2M

Two young gay men, sitting at the bar of their usual haunt, observe and discuss their many past sexual conquests that come and go before them throughout the evening over a cocktail…and perhaps a drink.

Cocktail Conversation premiered at the Producers Club in New York in 2002.

CHARACTERS

MIKE: Amiable. Not as confident as he'd like to appear. 20s/30s.

JIM: Mordant sense of humor. Somewhat jaded in attitude. 20s/30s.

SETTING & TIME

SETTING: A gay bar or club.

TIME: Night. The present.

At Rise: *Two young men sit at a bar in a gay pub, each cradling a glass in his hands. Both appear less than enthused as they idly observe the various people who come and go before them at a point somewhere beyond the fourth wall. As each unseen patron passes their field of view – from left to right and vice versa – their heads follow, sometimes in unison, as they offer their critiques.*

MIKE: (*His eyes following someone across the room.*) Done him.

JIM: Done him.

    (*Pause. Another passer-by crosses their view.*)

MIKE: Done him.

JIM: Yep, done him.

    (*Pause. Another passer-by crosses their view.*)

MIKE: Done him, as well.

JIM: Yeah, done him, too.

    (*Pause. Another passer-by crosses their view.*)

MIKE: I've *definitely* done him.

JIM: Who hasn't done him?

> (*Pause. MIKE takes something from his shirt pocket and puts it in his mouth, swallows it and washes down with a swig from his glass. Another passer-by crosses their view.*)

MIKE: Not sure if I've done him. (*Beat.*) Looks familiar, though.

JIM: I've done him.

MIKE: Have you?

JIM: Oh, yeah. Done him not long ago, as a matter of fact.

MIKE: Have I done him?

JIM: How should I know? Ask him.

MIKE: Think I've done him…I'm just not sure. (*Beat.*) Well, you've done him – if I haven't done him should I do him?

JIM: (*With a shrug.*) Up to you. Personally I wouldn't do him again.

MIKE: Mmm.

> (*Pause. This time JIM takes something from his shirt pocket and puts it in his mouth, swallows it and washes down with a swig from his glass. Another passer-by crosses their view.*)

MIKE: Now, I've done him a few times.

JIM: I done him once, but…God knows when. Years ago,

that's for sure.

MIKE: One time five of us did him at once.

JIM: Tight squeeze.

MIKE: Very funny.

JIM: That explains it, then.

MIKE: Explains what?

JIM: Why he walks like that.

MIKE: Like what?

JIM: Like Donald Duck.

MIKE: No, he always walked like that. I think he thinks it makes people think he's got a big cock.

JIM: Does he?

MIKE: 'Course not, that's why he does it. If there was truth in advertising he'd be pigeon-toed.

JIM: You'd think I'd remember, wouldn't you? Aren't I awful?

MIKE: Aren't we all?

(*Pause. MIKE, again, takes something from his shirt pocket and puts it in his mouth, swallows it and washes down with a swig from his glass. Another passer-by crosses their view.)*

JIM: (*Mischievously.*) Have you done him?

MIKE: (*Beat.*) I don't remember.

JIM: So you have done him?

MIKE: I said I don't remember. (*Beat.*) And if I have done him it was probably because I was depressed...and bored...and couldn't find anything to wear that made me feel attractive to the same sex...and 'cause I looked in the mirror that morning and saw the first signs of my face losing its natural elasticity...and 'cause I'd left my contact lenses in the cleaning solution too long which meant I couldn't wear them that night which meant I was half blind...and 'cause that day that bitch Janice at work told me I looked like I was "filling out" which was her way of saying I looked like a fat pig who'd be more at home stuck on a spit roasting over an open fire, which completely sapped my confidence and is exactly where she should be, with the flames licking up around those ugly Marks-&-fucking-Spencer business suits she prances around in! (*Beat.*) But...like I say...I'm not saying I have done him – I just don't remember.

JIM: (*Gleefully.*) I knew it!

MIKE: And you haven't?

JIM: Sorry, dream boat, you're on your own there. (*Beat.*) Oh, no.

MIKE: What?

JIM: Your old shag – look what she's doing.

MIKE: Oh, no.

JIM: If she thinks for one second that bumming a light from Mr. Pecs is going to land her a night in Studsville she is sadly mistaken.

MIKE: Sadly mistaken.

JIM: Doomed to failure.

MIKE: Doomed.

(*Pause.*)

JIM: (*Fatalistically.*) There…blown off like a wet sperm fart.

MIKE: Some people just have no concept of what league they belong in.

JIM: Perhaps she was hoping Mr. Pecs had forgotten his contacts.

MIKE: I said I don't remember – remember?

JIM: Mmm…well, I'll say this much for her, she obviously manages to save money by not spending on clothes.

MIKE: Mmm…or matches.

JIM: Mmm.

> (*Pause. MIKE, again, takes something from his shirt pocket and puts it in his mouth, swallows it and washes down with a swig from his glass. Another passer-by crosses their view.*)

MIKE: Done him.

JIM: Of course you've done him – everyone's done him. I wouldn't be surprised if he hasn't done himself.

MIKE: I did him once with his girlfriend watching.

JIM: Girlfriend?

MIKE: Yeah, back when he was, you know…trying to pass.

JIM: Pass as what?

MIKE: Who knows?

JIM: What could you possibly pass as with a hair-do like that?

MIKE: Search me.

JIM: A former member of Duran Duran, maybe?

MIKE: Possibly.

JIM: And what did she think?

MIKE: Who?

JIM: The girlfriend.

MIKE: Couldn't tell you. She was completely strung out on...something. All I remember is her snapping her fingers out of time and singing the chorus of "Love is a Battlefield" over and over again.

JIM: Pat Benatar?

MIKE: Mmm.

JIM: Sad.

MIKE: Sad.

> (*Pause. Another passer-by crosses their view.*)

JIM: Done him.

MIKE: Yep, done him.

> (*Pause. JIM, again, takes something from his shirt pocket and puts it in his mouth, swallows it and washes down with a swig from his glass. Another passer-by crosses their view.*)

MIKE: Done that one.

JIM: (*With great skepticism.*) Yeah!

MIKE: What do you mean by that?

JIM: I mean, "Yeah!"

MIKE: Are you calling me a liar?

JIM: Not a liar, no, but…that's Miss Love Story.

MIKE: Who?

JIM: Miss "I won't have sex with anyone unless it means something."

MIKE: Well, I had sex with him.

JIM: Perhaps she's in love with you?

MIKE: So you are calling me a liar?

JIM: Look, I just know for a fact that she won't have sex with just anyone.

MIKE: Me being "just anyone"?

JIM: Of course you are. So am I. And I know from experience that she's extremely picky.

MIKE: Too picky to pick me according to you.

JIM: Maybe.

MIKE: Well, maybe you should make a note of this, Mr. Love Story-less: that is his routine.

JIM: What is?

MIKE: That whole, "It has to mean something to me" routine. Just like my, "Oh, you seemed so straight-looking, I thought you must've come here by mistake" routine, and your, "I'm actually married with three kids at home, but don't tell anyone" routine. It's how he operates.

JIM: Oh…huh! (*Beat.*) Sorry.

MIKE: Half-hearted apology accepted.

> (*Pause. MIKE, again, takes something from his shirt pocket and puts it in his mouth, swallows it and washes down with a swig from his glass. Another passer-by crosses their view.*)

JIM: Done him, done him, done him, God, I don't know how many times! How ever does he find the nerve to show his face down here?

MIKE: The same way you do, I expect.

JIM: I said I was sorry.

MIKE: Apology accepted – again.

> (*Beat.*)

JIM: He has a third nipple, you know.

MIKE: Does he? Where?

JIM: Between his third and fourth ribs on the left-hand side – if you're going upwards.

MIKE: I always go upwards. (*Beat.*) Three nipples...fancy that.

JIM: You've never done one with three nipples?

MIKE: Not that I'm aware of.

JIM: It's more common than you'd think.

MIKE: You live and learn, don't you? Could be quite fun, I suppose.

JIM: Well, call me old-fashioned but I still prefer just the two, otherwise I get this weird feeling I'm fucking a distant cousin of The Elephant Man or The Bearded Lady.

MIKE: Listen to you, you old-fashioned softy.

JIM: Bit of a passion killer...for me, at least.

MIKE: But only a "bit," apparently.

JIM: Well, I'd spent a long time working on him, hadn't I? I wasn't about to pack it in just because an extra nipple appeared on the scene. So, I took a deep breath and...packed it in.

MIKE: I thought you said you'd done him "God knows how many times"?

JIM: (*With a shrug.*) Well...it's like that song, "I've Grown Accustomed to his Face" – I grew accustomed to his extra nipple.

MIKE: That was a sweet thing to say.

JIM: Thank you.

> (*Pause. Another passer-by crosses their view.*)

JIM: (*Sympathetically.*) Ahhh...poor thing.

MIKE: I know...it's sad.

JIM: Still, let's not get down. She'll find someone...one of these days.

MIKE: One of these days.

> (*Pause. Both MIKE and JIM take something from their shirt pocket and put it in their mouth, swallow it and wash it down with a swig from their glass. Another passer-by crosses their view.*)

MIKE: (*Affronted.*) Oh, just look at him!

JIM: I am – every bit of him.

MIKE: You know I done him?

JIM: (*In disbelief.*) You did not.

MIKE: Before he was even legal.

JIM: I hate you!

MIKE: Well, don't hate me that much – that was when he was still in his "I'm not sure what I am" phase. It was all very awkward and unsatisfying. Now look at him: the "it man"…the belle of the ball. He makes me sick.

JIM: Mmm…even so.

MIKE: (*Upon reflection.*) Yeah…even so.

> (*Pause. Another passer-by crosses their view.*)

JIM: Ooh, look at that. I'd do him in a New York minute.

MIKE: That's all you'd need.

JIM: You've done him?

MIKE: Briefly.

JIM: I don't care. Someone like that, I'd just be happy to bathe my eyes in his beautiful, criminal, physical perfection. (*Beat.*) That, and shove my cock up his ass as hard as I could.

MIKE: You are in a silly, romantic mood this evening, aren't you?

JIM: Must've been all that talk about Miss Love Story.

> (*Pause. JIM, again, takes something from his shirt pocket and puts it in his mouth, swallows it and washes down with a swig*

from his glass. Another passer-by crosses their view.)

MIKE: Not if you paid me.

JIM: Not if you paid me either…unless it was a lot.

MIKE: What do you call a lot?

JIM: I don't know…a lot.

MIKE: Like what?

JIM: A hell of a lot.

MIKE: A thousand?

JIM: Oh, fuck off!

MIKE: Well, what then?

JIM: I don't know.

MIKE: Ten thousand?

JIM: I don't know.

MIKE: A hundred thousand?

JIM: Well, of course a hundred thousand.

MIKE: You'd do that for a hundred thousand?

JIM: You wouldn't?

MIKE: For a hundred thousand...probably.

JIM: What do you mean, "probably"? You'd fuck it like it was Tom Cruise if you knew there was a hundred grand at the other end.

MIKE: What end?

JIM: His end.

MIKE: Wouldn't you?

JIM: Of course I would.

MIKE: So, what's your point?

JIM: It was your point.

MIKE: Point taken.

(*Pause. Another passer-by crosses their view.*)

JIM: Done him.

MIKE: Yeah, done him.

(*Pause. JIM, again, takes something from his shirt pocket and puts it in his mouth, swallows it and washes down with a swig from his glass. Another passer-by crosses their view.*)

MIKE: Done that one, too.

JIM: (*Apathetically.*) Yep, done.

> (*Pause. MIKE, again, takes something from his shirt pocket and puts it in his mouth, swallows it and washes down with a swig from his glass. Another passer-by crosses their view.*)

MIKE: Oh, look…there's Pork Tenderloin.

JIM: Who?

MIKE: Pork Tenderloin.

JIM: What do you call him that for?

MIKE: Only takes meat if it comes shrink-wrapped in plastic.

JIM: Once upon a time, maybe – not any more. These days he gets it fresh from the butchers.

MIKE: How would you know?

JIM: 'Cause I done him.

MIKE: Shrink-wrapped?

JIM: Nope.

MIKE: You must've been. He's very fussy. Famous for it.

JIM: (*Emphatically.*) I've done him.

MIKE: Bareback?

JIM: Bareback.

MIKE: Well, either he knows something that you don't know, or I know something that he doesn't.

JIM: What?

MIKE: Either…actually, I'm not sure now. I think I've confused myself.

JIM: Look, it was no big deal. I just explained to him that if he'd never done it skinless then he'd never really done it 'cause it feels completely different, and that, anyway, it doesn't really matter who's positive and who's not these days, 'cause whatever happens – with the right drug combo – you can virtually live forever.

MIKE: Then he said yes?

JIM: Then he said, "Who'd wanna do that?"

MIKE: What a funny thing to say. Was he depressed?

JIM: Couldn't tell you.

MIKE: So, then you did him?

JIM: Then I did him.

MIKE: The pink pound?

JIM: The pink pound.

MIKE: Fuck, if I'd known it was that easy I'd have done him long ago. (*Beat.*) Finished your cocktail?

JIM: (*As he reaches into his shirt pocket.*) Two more…hang on.

> (*JIM swallows the last of his pills and takes a swig from his glass, as MIKE reaches inside of his own shirt pocket.*)

JIM: Finished yours?

MIKE: (*Still feeling about in his pocket.*) Yep…nope …one more.

> (*MIKE swallows his last pill and washes it down with a swig from his glass.*)

JIM: See anything worth doing?

MIKE: Not tonight.

JIM: Got your contacts in?

MIKE: Yeah.

JIM: Wanna do me?

MIKE: Might as well.

> (*MIKE and JIM get up to leave.*)

JIM: Aren't you going to finish your water?

MIKE: I don't like water.

JIM: Please yourself.

> (*MIKE and JIM begin to leave. MIKE suddenly stops.*)

MIKE: Wait…my cigarettes.

> (*MIKE steps back to the bar and retrieves his cigarettes.*)

JIM: I thought you were giving that up, anyway?

MIKE: I am…just not yet.

JIM: (*With a shrug.*) Your funeral.

> (*They exit as the lights fade to BLACKOUT.*)

END OF PLAY

The Joneses

THE JONESES

1M/1F

In this decidedly dark comedy, Mr. and Mrs. Jones' zealous desire to be seen as doyens of the community leads them to undertake a misguided mission that rapidly spirals out of control. However, in spite of the grim realities that now confront them, they remain stalwart in their pursuit of a higher social standing. But is that really the smell of victory in the air...or did things just get a little too hot to handle?

The Joneses was a semi-finalist in the 11th Annual National One-Act Play Competition by First Stage in Hollywood, CA in 2007.

CHARACTERS

MR. JONES: Intransigent, pragmatic, with a zealous edge. 30s/50s.

MRS. JONES: Highly-strung, with a somewhat affected manner, occasionally revealing an inner resentment. 30s/50s.

SETTING & TIME

SETTING: A living room.

TIME: The recent past.

At Rise: MR. JONES .is sitting in an armchair, Stage R., his head buried in a newspaper. Presently, MRS. JONES enters from Stage L. in an extremely agitated state, slamming the door behind her.

MRS. JONES: That's it! I've had enough! They've tried my patience one too many times today and now I've just about had it! There's nothing more I can do – I give up!

MR. JONES: (*Without looking up.*) Something wrong, Mrs. Jones?

MRS. JONES: It doesn't matter what I say, nothing makes a blind bit of difference. I may as well be talking to a brick wall.

MR. JONES: Is it the children again?

MRS. JONES: Of course it's the children. When is it not the children? I never get a minute's peace with those two. It's one long constant battle of wills.

MR. JONES: Well I'm sure they'll soon settle down if you just let them be for a while.

MRS. JONES: Let them be? How on earth am I supposed to do that when they're hell bent on beating the living daylights out of each other?

MR. JONES: Boys will be boys, Mrs. Jones. You can't expect

them to behave like model children all of the time.

MRS. JONES: I just need a little peace and quiet. Is that really so much to ask?

MR. JONES: Parenthood brings with it all manner of responsibilities, some of them none too pleasant. We'd acknowledged and agreed that it wasn't likely to be all plain sailing long before we made the decision to adopt.

MRS. JONES: I am fully aware of what my responsibilities are, thank you all the same. But I wonder, Mr. Jones…are you?

MR. JONES: What are you implying?

MRS. JONES: Well, you're supposed to be the man of the house, aren't you? Why don't you try doing something about it, instead of just sitting there ogling the sports pages?

MR. JONES: Perhaps because I know when to leave well enough alone. Mark my words, it'll all blow over if you just let them sort it out amongst themselves.

> (*Just then several loud sounds of things crashing and banging are heard offstage.*)

MRS. JONES: Oh how right you are. The spirit of reconciliation never sounded sweeter. My apologies for ever doubting your word.

MR. JONES: I fail to see how resorting to sarcasm is going to improve matters.

MRS. JONES: But what are we going to do, for heaven's sake? We can't just let them pulverize each other into the ground.

MR. JONES: I think you're making rather more of this than is absolutely necessary.

MRS. JONES: But listen to what they're doing to each other in there! They're not just unruly, they're unhinged. We are their parents. We have a responsibility for their safety and wellbeing, and what's happening in that room right now is simply not normal!

MR. JONES: May I remind you, Mrs. Jones, that our little darlings originate from a gene pool of which we know absolutely nothing about. Moreover, the culture from which we rescued them is vastly different to our own, and I think it behooves us to remain sensitive to some of their ethnic idiosyncrasies, however cruel they may appear to us. For all we know, this may be their way of bonding. And as much as we may desire to bestow our superior lifestyle upon them, we have to accept that they're going to have their little ways.

(Just then, more loud crashes and bangs are heard offstage.)

MRS. JONES: Little ways? That's putting it mildly. *(Sitting in the armchair L.)* I had no idea motherhood would be so traumatizing.

MR. JONES: Well what is it they're fighting about exactly?

235

What's the problem here?

MRS. JONES: Oh, I don't know – it's always something different. Then again, it all amounts to the same thing. Last week it was the bunk bed. Ali, being a year older, decided that he should be the one in the top bunk. Omar, having gotten used to being there, refused to budge. Pandemonium and mayhem ensued, of course, until finally Ali got his way. Now Omar's refusing to share the same room with him and it's become a full-scale conflict to see who can force the other out. They've taken to strangling each other in the middle of the night.

MR. JONES: Then perhaps you're not thinking far enough outside of the box. Why don't you suggest to them that they divide the room into separate sections, each with its own half of the bunk? That way they can both feel important.

MRS. JONES: It wouldn't make a jot of difference. It's not about sharing, it's about control. Omar wants Ali out and vice versa. Each thinks the other should sleep in the study from hereon, and both seem willing to stop at nothing in order to make that a reality.

MR. JONES: I am not having my study turned into a bedroom! That is sacred ground! Some of my greatest thinking is done in that room.

MRS. JONES: Oh calm down. No one's asking you to give up your study, I'm just trying to illustrate the gravity of a situation that, whether through negligence or wantonness, you have thus far seemed completely oblivious to.

(*More loud smashing and banging is heard offstage.*)

MR. JONES: (*Cautiously.*) Then I think the time may have come for us to consider employing a little d-i-s-c-i-p-l-i-n-e.

MRS. JONES: You needn't bother spelling it out. They can't hear you from here, they wouldn't understand, and more to the point, they wouldn't care, either. Trust me, I've tried every means at my disposal and nothing seems to make an impact. The minute I turn my head they're back at it again.

MR. JONES: (*Reprovingly.*) Spare the rod, spoil the child, Mrs. Jones, that's how I was raised.

MRS. JONES: I haven't spared the rod! Good God, I've yelled and screamed at them until I've made myself hoarse, but it doesn't make the slightest difference.

MR. JONES: What about a curfew?

MRS. JONES: (*With an air of exasperation.*) Doesn't work, I've tried it. I've locked them in their room, I've put pillowcases over their heads, I've bound their wrists and ankles together with jump rope, I've made them stand on their lunchboxes for hours at a time until their muscles gave out, I've even set the dog on them. I mean, what else is a mother supposed to do? Tell me!

MR. JONES: Now, now, don't get yourself all worked into a state. Just like anything else, child rearing has its obstacles, but I'm quite sure it'll all sort itself out if we keep our heads and stop focusing on the negative all the time.

MRS. JONES: You keep saying that, but I can't help having this nagging suspicion that we've bitten off far more than we can chew.

MR. JONES: That's defeatist talk and I will hear no more of it. A firm hand and a steely jaw are all that's needed to prevail, just you wait and see.

(MRS. JONES rises and begins nervously pacing the room.)

MRS. JONES: Oh, I suppose you're right. I don't know what to think anymore. It's just that I'd had such high hopes for all of this. I'd always imagined our neighbors looking upon us as the ultimate parents, setting an example of just what can be accomplished when two privileged, determined individuals wrap their arms around a couple of scraggly little souls from some barbaric outpost of humanity and turn them into something shiny and new. *(With a sigh.)* It sounds silly now, but I'd even dreamt of being looked upon as something of a visionary; of my name being mentioned only in the most hushed and hallowed of tones. *(Beat.)* Now I fear we'll be seen as nothing more than two meddling, bungling fools who orchestrated a disaster, all in the name of their own vanity. Oh, what have we done, Mr. Jones? What have we done?

MR. JONES: Stop talking like that! I won't hear of it. I refuse to let the antics of a couple of scruffy little Third World sand rats taint our standing and reputation in this community as generous, warm-hearted benefactors. Now, there are bound to be bumps in the road – that's only to be expected. But we cannot allow a little over-excitedness on the part of our beloved children to throw off our moral compass. After all, at the end of the day it's just a little sibling rivalry.

MRS. JONES: Perhaps that's half the problem? Perhaps if we'd picked two from the same family we wouldn't be having to endure all of this mayhem.

MR. JONES: Well, it's too late now. We can't start second guessing ourselves. What's done is done.

MRS. JONES: And I'd hardly call it "sibling rivalry." Last week I caught Ali drilling holes in Omar's leg with your Black & Decker drill. The week before, I discovered Omar…well, I'd rather not go into it before dinner. Suffice to say that every time I take them to the emergency room, I find the hospital staff giving me stranger and stranger looks. I'd almost say they were accusatory…as if I were somehow to blame.

MR. JONES: Then perhaps it's time we thought about bringing in some help; someone who can share the blame. I mean, er…the responsibility.

MRS. JONES: You mean like a nanny or an au pair?

MR. JONES: Yes. Someone cheap from abroad.

MRS. JONES: But I thought I told you – I interviewed several qualified individuals last week for just such a position and none of them were interested. They took one look at Omar and Ali having at it and bolted for the door.

MR. JONES: Damn! All of them?

MRS. JONES: Well, there was one willing to offer her services – a rather gruesome looking woman from Uzbekistan with hairy forearms – but quite frankly her terms were outlandish.

MR. JONES: Then to hell with them! We'll go it alone, just you and me. We'll show them all.

MRS. JONES: Easy for you to say, you're the one with his head buried in the sports pages half the day. I'm the one out there on the front lines having to deal with this madness.

(More banging sounds, followed by a bloodcurdling scream.)

MR. JONES: And you've been doing a spectacular job, Mrs. Jones. No one could be more proud of you than I am. But I think it's worth remembering that adopting children is a very big undertaking. It's not quite the same as having a pet – you can't simply send them back to the shelter once they start making puddles on the carpet.

MRS. JONES: *(With a deep sigh.)* Oh, sometimes I just wish we could. I know it's awful to admit, but it's true.

MR. JONES: It's also completely impossible, so I suggest you banish the thought from your mind at the earliest opportunity.

MRS. JONES: *(With a slightly bitter tone.)* I know it's impossible. *(Beat.)* I also recall the reason why.

MR. JONES: I see. So we're back to throwing that in my

face, are we?

MRS. JONES: I'm not throwing anything in your face; I was simply reminding myself that I was not the one with a history of substance abuse.

MR. JONES: For the umpteenth time, Mrs. Jones, it was a foible of youth!

MRS. JONES: Yes, and one that got us turned down by every legitimate adoption agency in Christendom.

MR. JONES: Mr. Qasim's services were entirely professional and utterly beyond reproach. I read all of his references and I still maintain we had no reason to doubt him.

MRS. JONES: Clearly not. Look, why don't we just face the truth – we were willing to accept just about anything that conniving little crook told us, however ludicrous, because we were so damned desperate to get our hands on those children and prove something to the world. (*Beat.*) And now look at us…a laughing stock.

> (*Just then an enormous crash is heard, along with the sound of breaking glass, followed by another bloodcurdling scream.*)

MR. JONES: (*Standing abruptly.*) We are *not* a laughing stock, we are *not* defeatists, and we *will* make this work. Together, you and I are going to demonstrate to our dear friends and neighbors just exactly what it is that makes us superior to them. Oh, I know they're all peeking from behind their curtains, just waiting for us to fail. I hear all the snickering and the sniping and the muttering of "I told you so" under their breath. Don't think it passes me by. But they'll be smiling on the other side of their faces by the time we're through. Mark my words, between you, me and the good grace of the Almighty, we're going to make those bastards eat shit.

(*MRS. JONES crosses to her husband and puts her arms around him.*)

MRS. JONES: Oh, Mr. Jones, do you really think it's possible?

MR. JONES: (*With a resolute outward gaze.*) It's more than possible, it's inevitable. It's destiny.

MRS. JONES: I do so hope you're right. When you first suggested all of this to me, I must confess I did have my misgivings. But I tried to hide them because I...because I wanted to make you happy, and because...well, because a part of me felt inadequate, if you must know. I felt ashamed because I couldn't give you those children. (*Beat.*) There was a time, of course, way back when, in the days when I was still young and vital...when it seemed as though the sun would never set. But when I met you it was already too late. I was already past my prime. Just a barren trophy wife from a good family with a respected name.

MR. JONES: A damned fine name. You gave me instant cachet. I couldn't have asked for better.

MRS. JONES: (*With a loving embrace.*) And neither could I.

Suddenly it seemed as if all my schoolgirl dreams had come true. There I was, about to be married to the wealthiest, most powerful man in the community. And I knew that together we'd be even stronger. This was not going to be any run-of-the-mill union of two people, this was…this was something special.

MR. JONES: Very special.

MRS. JONES: Everyone could tell.

MR. JONES: They knew it.

MRS. JONES: And when the children came along – well, when we procured them – I thought that our stature would only be enhanced, as if that were possible. I imagined people to be awestruck by our largesse; to marvel at our determination to share everything we cherish and hold dear with two impoverished little urchins from the lands of the mystics. (*Beat.*) Could it really all have been a dream just out of reach?

MR. JONES: Ah, but dreams need to be believed in if you wish to keep them alive. You keep rounding back to reality, Mrs. Jones, but no good will come of it. Believe me, it's a mistake.

> (*Suddenly more deafening noise is heard, followed by several gunshots and a sickening scream.*)

MRS. JONES: But just listen to them, Mr. Jones. That is not the sound of a happy home.

MR. JONES: It's the sound of change. Pay them no mind – you just keep dreaming the dream.

MRS. JONES: (*Becoming tearful.*) Could it be that we've…we've failed as parents?

MR. JONES: No! Now just you listen to me. We have given those wild-eyed little carpetbaggers the opportunity of a lifetime. Before we intervened in their lives they were living some miserable, hand-to-mouth existence in that godforsaken, armpit of a country, under the tutelage of shamans. What we did for those boys was nothing short of a miracle. Good God, Mrs. Jones, there are literally millions of dark-skinned little wretches roaming the savannahs of Africa that would have offered up a limb to have what they have. But no, we chose Omar and Ali…and this is the thanks we get. So I say to hell with them! Let them sort it out for themselves. We've done all we can.

MRS. JONES: But we can't just abandon them. It would be pure chaos in there.

(*MR. JONES throws her a look of irony.*)

MRS. JONES: (*Wearily.*) Well…I suppose it does seem rather ungrateful.

MR. JONES: Ungrateful? It's the height of ignorance. Let them beat each other to a pulp. They can rip each other to shreds for all I care. This mess is as much their responsibility as it is ours and it's high time they took ownership. If they don't learn now they never will.

MRS. JONES: And it's true we can only guide them so far, after all.

MR. JONES: Personal responsibility, Mrs. Jones.

MRS. JONES: And I suppose these things do have a way of sorting themselves out sometimes.

MR. JONES: Of course they do. You just have to give it time. It all comes right in the end. You just have to keep believing. Keep the dream alive, Mrs. Jones. Live the dream. Live and breathe it. Let it fill your mind.

MRS. JONES: Yes, I…I am beginning to feel a little fuzzy, actually.

MR. JONES: That's it, that's the spirit – open yourself up to it.

MRS. JONES: No, I mean…I'm starting to feel a bit odd. (*Sniffing the air.*) Do you smell something?

MR. JONES: I don't smell a thing.

MRS. JONES: It…it smells like smoke. (*Sniffing the air again.*) Is something burning?

> (*Very gradually the lights slowly begin turning redder and redder.*)

MR. JONES: The only thing that's burning is the beacon of hope that you and I have lit for our blessed children.

MRS. JONES: It definitely smells like smoke to me.

MR. JONES: (*Clutching her to his side and pointing out ahead.*) Look to the light, Mrs. Jones, and believe in its promise of a brighter tomorrow. There's a new sun rising on a world where everything is right again, and we shall bask in its warmth and glory.

MRS. JONES: Yes, it...it is starting to get a little warm in here. Are you sure you can't smell anything?

> (*The crackling sounds of a fire can be heard, as the lights grow increasingly redder.*)

MR. JONES: It's the smell of victory, Mrs. Jones. It's the smell of all our naysaying neighbors eating their words. It's the smell of every malcontent and turncoat friend fuming at the prospect of our glorious success as proud parents. Breathe it in – breathe it deep into your lungs!

MRS. JONES: (*After a deep breath, followed by a coughing fit.*) It's...it's rather pungent, isn't it? (*Between coughs.*) I say, those...those boys are awfully quiet. I do hope they're not...not making mischief.

MR. JONES: Why worry about them? Just look! Look to the light! Have you ever seen a sight more magnificent? Just look at it – bursting with the hope of a brighter future. Give into it, Mrs. Jones. Accept it. Breathe it in, breathe it in deep. Have you ever smelled anything so intoxicating?

MRS. JONES: (*Coughing heavily.*) No, I...I...actually, I...oh...

(MRS. JONES faints and drops to the floor. MR. JONES raises his arms to the sky, the lights flooding the stage with red, the sound of flames growing ever louder.)

MR. JONES: Yes, Mrs. Jones, throw yourself before Him! Oh thank you, Lord! Thank you for this unshakeable will you've given us. Thank you for bestowing upon us the strength and determination to stand firm in the face of the incredulous. Your words have been my weapons. I am yours, your humble servant, your vessel, your instrument of change. My children are now your children, freed from the grasp of the wailing pagans, free to embrace their new life. And we'll help them; we'll teach them and tame them. Oh, how happy they'll be! Educated and integrated, anglicised and circumcised. They'll dance and sing and praise the day the heavens opened up and changed their world forever. Oh, what model children they'll be, such model children. An example to the world! And they will call me father, and they will take my name, and they will be my legacy when I am gone, these children of the sand. Oh thank you, dear Lord, for leading me on this path, for bringing me to this place. I feel you here. I feel the warmth of your breath, the fire of your passion, the red hot glow of your unending embrace. *(Beat.)* I am with you now, here where I belong. I've come home...home to you.*(Beat.)* You knew I'd come. And I knew you'd be waiting...waiting here for me. *(Beat.)* Waiting with your baptismal fires; your eternal flames. Waiting in that light that never goes out...never goes out.

(The lights fade to BLACK.)

END OF PLAY

Tacked-On Ending

TACKED-ON ENDING

2M

It's the end of the evening and two actors pack up their belongings and prepare to leave the theatre. While one of them felt the show went great, the other is left with the uneasy feeling that the final scene didn't quite deliver. Was his performance to blame, or was it the play's deus ex machina, which is not only highly implausible but also oddly familiar?

CHARACTERS

ACTOR 1: An actor from the play you've just seen. Age open.

ACTOR 2: Another actor from the play you've just seen. Age open.

SETTING & TIME

SETTING: Backstage.

TIME: The present.

At rise: ACTOR 1 is discovered picking up his various belongings and putting them into a bag. Presently, ACTOR 2 enters from stage L., a backpack slung over his shoulder.

ACTOR 2: Heading out?

ACTOR 1: Yep...yep.

ACTOR 2: *(Scanning the room)* I thought I left my... *(Beat)* Huh...I guess I didn't.

ACTOR 1: What?

ACTOR 2: Oh, nothing. Just losing my mind, that's all.

(Pause.)

ACTOR 1: Great audience tonight.

ACTOR 2: Oh yeah, fantastic. Stellar.

ACTOR 1: Not like last night's.

ACTOR 2: *Oh*...oh, don't even remind me. What the hell was wrong with that lot? Miserable bastards.

ACTOR 1: Beats me. Still, tonight's made up for it.

ACTOR 2: Damn right – and then some. They were loving everything I was doing out there. How about you? Felt good?

ACTOR 1: Well…I mean…yeah…I mean…yeah…more or less. It's just that…

ACTOR 2: What?

ACTOR 1: Well…I mean…it was good, all of it, it just…well, just right at the very end, it just…something…it just felt a bit off, d'ya know what I mean?

ACTOR 2: Yeah, endings are tricky. 'Course, I'm not in the last scene, so it's not really my problem.

ACTOR 1: Well, no, and…and the thing is…well…I mean…I don't wanna sound arrogant or anything, 'cause I'm not, I mean, you know me.

ACTOR 2: Oh, yeah, no, no.

ACTOR 1: But it was definitely off, and the thing is, it usually is…and the thing is, you know, like…I'm not sure if it's me…or the play.

ACTOR 2: Huh.

ACTOR 1: 'Cause, I mean, you know…I'm a classically trained actor.

ACTOR 2: Right, right.

ACTOR 1: I mean, I've had private coaching from McKellen.

ACTOR 2: (*Taken aback*) McKellen?

ACTOR 1: Oh, yeah.

ACTOR 2: Well, that's certainly impressive.

ACTOR 1: Yeah, yeah – he's very good.

ACTOR 2: You don't have to tell me. (*Musing*) Fancy that, private coaching from Sir Ian McKellen.

ACTOR 1: Oh, no...not that one.

ACTOR 2: What?

ACTOR 1: Not Ian – John.

ACTOR 2: John?

ACTOR 1: Yeah, John McKellen. He rents one of those studios over on Gower Street. He's very good. Very, very good.

ACTOR 2: Oh...right.

ACTOR 1: Anyway, the thing is...I know my stuff, you know?

ACTOR 2: Yeah, 'course you do.

ACTOR 1: But just at the end – and I have no idea why – something just always seems to ring a bit…false.

ACTOR 2: Well, like I said, you know – endings are tricky things. Sometimes they just sort of lazily drift off, leaving everything up in the air; other times, they get wrapped up all too conveniently by a bus load of silly coincidences that leave you with the feeling that you've just been ripped off; and then other times…well, other times they just feel a bit…tacked-on, you know?

ACTOR 1: Tacked-on? How do you mean?

ACTOR 2: You know, like a…what's it called? A deus ex machina.

ACTOR 1: A what?

ACTOR 2: A deus ex machina. It's a plot device that writers use – presumably when they're at a complete and utter loss of how to finish what they started.

ACTOR 1: But what is it?

ACTOR 2: Well, it's, you know, it's where they suddenly introduce some completely unexpected event or person or whatever that changes the whole scenario in one fell swoop and gets them out of the hole they've dug themselves into.

ACTOR 1: Sounds like a bit of a cop-out to me.

ACTOR 2: It is. And I've a feeling that that, my friend, may well be your problem.

ACTOR 1: Huh. (*Ponders*) Yeah...yeah, you might have a point there.

ACTOR 2: Remind me, if you will, how the play ends again.

ACTOR 1: You mean you don't know?

ACTOR 2: Hey, shoot me – I forgot, okay? I'm usually outta here after my last scene. I've got better things to do than stick around here all night.

ACTOR 1: All right, all right. I was just surprised, that's all.

ACTOR 2: All right, so?

ACTOR 1: So what?

ACTOR 2: (*Impatiently*) How does it end?

ACTOR 1: Oh, well...well, in the very last scene, my character's been left all by himself, so he decides it's time that he should be moving on, too, so he starts packing up his stuff into a bag.

ACTOR 2: Right.

ACTOR 1: But then, just as he's doing that, the guy from the earlier scenes – the one everyone thought had left forever – suddenly returns.

ACTOR 2: Right, right.

ACTOR 1: So, you know, they get to talking about this and that, the audience, stuff like that.

ACTOR 2: Yep, yep, go on.

ACTOR 1: And then comes this revelation. Well, sort of a revelation, I suppose.

ACTOR 2: Which is?

ACTOR 1: That my character doesn't feel that good about his, you know…his performance.

ACTOR 2: Ah, now this is definitely starting to sound familiar.

ACTOR 1: So the other guy starts telling him that maybe his performance isn't the problem, but the way the play ends.

ACTOR 2: Yes, yes, it's starting to come back to me now.

ACTOR 1: So then the guy starts telling him about some ludicrous plot device that writers sometimes use when they don't have a clue how to end their play.

ACTOR 2: A deus ex machina!

ACTOR 1: Yeah, that's it!

ACTOR 2: And then he realizes that the play has one?

ACTOR 1: Exactly.

(*Pause.*)

ACTOR 2: So what is it?

ACTOR 1: What?

ACTOR 2: The deus ex machina?

ACTOR 1: Oh, yeah…well, you see, when the other guy – the one everyone thought was gone forever but who then suddenly returns – well, when he was making his return journey, at some point during his travels, his wife's psychotic lover had somehow managed to plant a bomb inside his backpack.

ACTOR 2: Oh, come on! Oh, now that really is a cop-out. How ridiculous is that?

ACTOR 1: Yeah, I…I had my reservations, to be honest.

ACTOR 2: And what? The bomb goes off and they both get blown to pieces in some sort of inane tragedy, is that it?

ACTOR 1: More or less.

ACTOR 2: Well…there you are, then. There's your problem.

(*A ticking sound is heard.*)

ACTOR 1: Yeah…yeah, I think you might be right.

ACTOR 2: I know I am.

ACTOR 1: By the way.

(*The ticking sound becomes louder.*)

ACTOR 2: Yes.

ACTOR 1: What's that noise? Is your backpack ticking?

ACTOR 2: Yes, I believe it is. Why do you ask?

ACTOR 1: Well–

(*Suddenly the backpack explodes and they are both blown to pieces in some sort of inane tragedy.*)

END OF PLAY

ABOUT THE AUTHOR

From the Royal Court Theatre in London to the Playhouse Theatre in Tasmania, the works of award-winning playwright Andrew Biss have been performed across the globe, spanning four continents. His plays have won awards on both coasts of the U.S., critical acclaim in the U.K., and quickly became a perennial sight on Off and Off-Off Broadway stages.

In London his plays have been performed at The Royal Court Theatre, Theatre503, Riverside Studios, The Pleasance Theatre, The Union Theatre, The White Bear Theatre, The Brockley Jack Studio Theatre, Fractured Lines Theatre & Film at COG ARTSpace, and Ghost Dog Productions at The Horse & Stables.

In New York his plays have been produced at Theatre Row Studios, The Samuel French Off-Off-Broadway Festival, The Kraine Theater, The Red Room Theater, Times Square Arts Center, Manhattan Theatre Source, Mind The Gap Theatre, 3Graces Theatre Company, Emerging Artists Theatre, Curan Repertory Company, Pulse Ensemble Theatre, American Globe Theatre, The American Theater of Actors, and Chashama Theatres, among others.

His plays and monologues are published in numerous anthologies from trade publishers Bedford/St. Martin's, Smith & Kraus, Inc., Pioneer Drama Service, and Applause Theatre & Cinema Books.

Andrew is a graduate of the University of the Arts London, and a member of the Dramatists Guild of America, Inc.

For more information please visit his website at:

www.andrewbiss.com

RIGHTS AND PERMISSIONS

For information regarding performance rights, licensing and royalty arrangements for any of the plays included in this collection, please contact info@andrewbiss.com or fill out the contact form on the playwright's website at: www.andrewbiss.com/contact

Made in United States
Troutdale, OR
03/19/2024

TEN-MINUTE PLAYS

——— THE ———

COMEDY
COLLECTION